To Alegra
my fell

Miriam.

Myra

Myra
The Silent Child Who Found A Voice

By Miry Vicks

completelynovel.com

*To my children and grandchildren
and to the memory of George without whom I would
not be here to tell this story.*

Acknowledgements

This could not have been written without the help
and contribution of my friend and teacher Claudia
Gould, who used to rise her hands in despair at
my poor spelling and grammar
and a special thanks and gratitude to my close
friend Michael Reeves, also to all my friends from
the JWFS family history group.
Thank you for believing in me

1
BIRTH

Barlad, Romania, February 1939

'This baby isn't coming out!'

'It had better or I'll kill you, you drunken witch,' said Usher, fear shouting in his voice.

'Shut up, both of you,' Esther gasped when the pain gave her a chance to breathe. 'Go and see if you can bring the doctor. It isn't far. You can get through the snow.'

'Yes, make yourself useful, you moron,' the midwife muttered under her breath, her plump hands reaching for the bottle of plum brandy. 'If you don't want to bury her.'

With one hand she lifted Esther's head and with the other she pushed the neck of the bottle into her mouth, nearly choking her.

'Drink, you will feel better.' Then she took a swig herself to give her the strength she needed.

'Stop pushing,!' the midwife said. 'You'll split yourself open. Wait for the doctor to come and help.'

'I can't help it. What's the matter with this child? Doesn't it want to come out?'

'It doesn't. It's cosy and warm in there, perhaps it can feel how cold and frosty this February is. I wonder if Usher will make it, with this wind blowing, and the snowdrifts. And you here, poor mite, with no mother or sister to be by your side.'

Every now and again, Esther's screams pierced the air. The room grew colder and colder as the darkness fell. The midwife took the lamp down to the cellar to bring up some wood to put on the fire.

Esther was wondering if this was the end. She felt all alone with her unborn child.

That was how Myra was born. It wasn't Esther's time to die on that cold February night. The doctor appeared with Usher barely walking, almost frozen. The doctor gave the midwife a sharp look and rolled up his sleeves. He took a scalpel out of the silver dish he carried in his bag and without anaesthetic cut the opening so that the baby's head could come out. Esther was already numbed by the plum brandy which she had shared with the midwife.

The wind howled, matching Esther's screams. It created snowdrifts as high as the house. After a while it had stopped blowing . The snowdrifts were so high by the time the doctor finished stitching the cut that he stayed on till daylight. He joined Usher and the midwife, by now half asleep, in ' wetting the baby's head' as it was the custom.. Esther was left to rest exhausted, with her fading thoughts, wondering at this skinny creature with the large misshapen head, who had given her so much trouble from the start.

This was the story Esther told Myra over and over again in the long nights of the war. There were many nights of dread and loneliness they spent together, nights when Esther talked out loud, as if she were talking to herself. It was a while before Myra started to understand the words and even then not all of them and she felt it was all her fault.

.

Usher could not stop gazing at the baby. He could not wait to share the news with his mother. His mother Anna and his sister Clara lived a short way down the road in the old rambling house where Usher had grown up, raised by Anna, who had been widowed early. Usher dug through the frozen drifts, under the silver blue daggers of the merciless sun. First he took the doctor home. He would have loved to scream his happiness to the whole world, or at least to his neighbours, if he could have seen them through the tunnels of ice they all dug to create an access road. They moved in separate worlds, creating ways limited by ice walls. His brother Gutzu was already out smoking, his eyes drifting with no sign of recognition, oblivious of snow and ice. Was he still perhaps searching for his own wife and the child he had lost?

Anna and Clara were already up, their sewing machines turning to the rhythm of Clara's foot on the treadle. The air was warm and so full of dust, small pieces of multi-coloured thread floating in the air, that one could barely see inside. A large black pot was bubbling over the open fire and Anna was busy stirring the contents with a wooden ladle.

Clara, her mouth full of pins as usual, lifted her head from the frock she was making and blinked to greet her brother.

3

'It's a girl,' he blurted out, full of joy. Anna rushed to her son and hugged him. She was a small woman, thin, and for her to give her son a hug he had to bend down. Clara waved, unable to speak, her lips sealed tight round the pins she held, ready to mark the frock. Usher told the women the whole saga, embellishing it a little, and never failing to say how much he had helped.

'Now go and give the good news to your eldest brother,' his mother said.

'Just let me rest a while. My hands are numb from shovelling all that snow, my feet are frozen. Milou said he was coming with me to see the rabbi, to give the child a name and he said he would help me. I could do with some money…just for a while.'

He left the women and started walking towards Sharaga's Mill, where his brother was working. The mill was closed so he turned round and made his way towards Milou's house.

Milou was an important man, the accountant of the mill. He was respected by everybody, and most of all by his family. He was the chosen one. When his father died, he became the head of the family. Milou studied hard and made a good life for himself. He married young and had a daughter. Her name was Estelle. Milou saw it as his duty to help his mother and his brothers and sister.

Usher found the house half buried under snow. It was an imposing house. Two large pillars guarded the front door. The few entrance steps had already been cleared and the pile of snow to the side had turned to a block of ice in the night.

As usual, he was received in the entrance hall. Milou and his wife Giselle congratulated him and wished his wife the best of happiness but they did not ask Usher in. He was not invited to sit or warm up so after an awkward moment he said his goodbyes. He left breathing a sigh of relief. Meetings with his brother were never easy; there was a barrier of wealth and education between the two men.

He returned to his family, his wife and his child. He opened the door quietly in case Esther was asleep.

'What took you so long?' Esther asked. She was wide awake. Her blue eyes, surrounded by the dark marks of fatigue and tears, were wide open. 'I fed her,' she said. 'Now, take her away, it's your turn to look after her.'

Usher was only too willing. 'How beautiful she is,' he said, gazing lovingly at the baby.

'I'm glad you find her beautiful. To me she looks like a lobster-coloured skinny frog. How could I have given birth to this? You should hear her screaming! And look at her head! I hope that head will change its shape. It is so misshapen!'

'You're tired Esther,' said Usher. 'I'll look after her while you go to sleep.'

So the new life started. They named the baby Myra.

Esther took a long time to get over the pain, and bonding with the baby was slow to come.

Usher divided his time between his work at the timber yard and running back at his home and family.

He helped as much as he could. Those were hard times. War was threatening. Persecution of Jewish people was becoming more severe. Usher, who had already been dismissed from the army because he was Jewish, was afraid the timber yard would be closed or taken over. Money was in increasingly short supply. Arguments began between Esther, who was low after the trauma of giving birth and lonely in a strange town without her own family to give her support, and Usher, with his worries about where tomorrow's meals would come from. Esther never asked for help from her mother in law or Clara. She felt that she did not know them well enough, and that they had plenty to worry about, without her adding to the pool of tears and sorrow. She was hoping that her mother would come to be with her.

2
A NEW BEGINNING

One night the earth began to shake so hard it made the little bed move away from the window and crush against the table. The windows broke and glass scattered everywhere.

Half-dressed, Usher grabbed Myra. Esther followed with her red mackintosh thrown over her night-dress. She took Myra from Usher's arms, covered her with a shawl and started running. First they ran towards Anna's house, shouting names as they advanced in the dark, falling from time to time as the earth was unstable under their feet.

'Anna. Clara. Gutsou. Are you there?'

'Yes, we are all alive,' they heard Clara call.

A drizzly rain started and the wind and noise were unbearable. A few fires were burning, lighting the gloomy darkness. There was no way to continue, so they found a spot in an open field and sat down. Myra slept through it all, cosy and warm in her mother's lap, sheltered from the wind and rain by her mother's raincoat, an old mackintosh out of which rubber and sweat aromas mingled together. Later, over many years, when she needed comfort, that smell of her mother's coat would come back to her.

Shock followed shock. Trees were falling and rolling, some on fire. They remained in the open for two days and nights, until slowly they made their way home, to start clearing the rubble, assess the damage and count the dead.

Anna's house lost its roof and the yard was full of scraps of wood, broken glass and uprooted trees. Only Gutsou still sat motionless on a stone, searching the sky with dead eyes for the answers to his unanswered questions.

Anna started to pray, and then she uttered her prediction:

'The war is now upon us. Hitler won't leave us be. This earthquake is our warning. This is the end!' It was 1941.

It might have been the beginning of the end but for Esther it was a new beginning, her revelation. Myra slept all through the earthquake, but at one point Esther felt she had gone limp, and for a split second she felt a deep panic. She feared she had lost Myra, that the child had died when she had fallen onto the moving earth. In her terror she shook Myra, who opened her eyes, looked around, yawned and went back to sleep. Tears of happiness fell from Esther's eyes. At that moment she realised that her baby was the most precious thing that belonged to her, to her alone and the earth might shake, might try to destroy everything but her baby was alive.

Esther's face, what she looked like as she was running, those details had been erased from Myra's mind, she was too young to remember, but the smell of the mackintosh and the feel still lingered. The only impressions Myra retained of that time involved darkness, drizzly rain, dogs howling and her father's voice piercing the dark. In Jennifer Eggan's words it was: 'Like a song that one once knew and made you feel a certain way, without a title, artist or even a few bars to bring it back. Nevertheless it hovers somewhere in the mind.'

3
ESTHER

The family home, 39 Stroe Boloescu, did not suffer much damage. When they came back, the broken glass that littered the narrow garden had already been swept away by the Romanian captain's soldiers who were living in the front of the house. Luckily it was a solidly built house, a gift from Esther's brothers.

Esther always said that the house was her reward for the years of misery she suffered with her parents. She was the only girl of the five children Risl and Moishe had. Moishe was a carpenter from the north of Romania, who came south when called upon to help build a new Jewish orphanage. The story goes that his forefathers came from a staetl across the Prout – the river that separates Romania from the Ukraine – on horseback to avoid conscription in the Tzar's army. They settled in the northern town of Botoshani and generations later Moishe moved south with his work in the town of Focsani. The work took a few years and he settled down, bought a small house with a front room where he set up shop. The room opened onto a little stone-paved street near the market. Pescaria Veche in the town of Focsani was a good place, between a large inn and a pub.

He was a pious, stern man, used to being the master in his house. He spoke Romanian but Risl had never mastered the language, although she, like her husband was born there. She only spoke

Yiddish. Their children were all bright, but Moishe Staler, as he was known, decided to pull them out of school as soon as they completed four primary classes and send them to apprentice places. The only children allowed to continue their educations were the youngest, Leon, at the School of Commerce and the girl, Esther, at the professional school. Esther did brilliantly at school. She was determined to go further, to go to university.

Leave home and go to university? Rise above her station? So one would have to make an appointment to see her? That was out of the question. A woman's place, said Moishe, was in the home, helping her mother look after the house and her brothers. That was the beginning of Esther's disappointments. She stayed at home, sewing, washing and ironing the shirts for her father and brothers to wear to work next day. She helped her mother with all the other chores. She read a lot when she could: *Gone With the Wind*, AJ Cronin's *The Castle* and Pearl Buck's stories of faraway China were her favourite.

Once a week she went out to meet her old school friends and together they went to an afternoon dance. A young man, the brother of one of her friends, started to ask her to dance a little more frequently than usual, and she began to look forward to these outings.

Gossip started, as is to be expected in a small town, and it reached Esther's parents. One Sunday morning the young man came to visit. Moishe invited him - in not the most polite terms- to leave the house immediately. An almighty row followed, with tears and recriminations. Moishe asserted that he was the father who made the decisions and he would be the one to choose a man who was right for his daughter. After that Ester vowed never to marry, no matter what pressure was put on her.

Esther would never married Usher, would never have married at all, but she finally gave in to appease her parents. Even then, she would have refused him if she had been well that day. But on that day in 1936 she was ill with tonsillitis, a regular spring event for her. She had a raging fever, her throat was on fire and eating was like swallowing razor blades. That was the day her parents invited Usher home to meet Esther. Her illness did not persuade them to postpone his visit.

Esther could barely see her suitor through her runny eyes. He was about her age. He was not too tall – that was acceptable- because she was small and very self-conscious about it. Her parents had tried to marry her off to a man that her father approved of, a man with a 'situation' and observant of the Jewish faith. That was what they had instructed the *shotchenta*, the professional woman match-maker to arrange. That meant a man who had a stable source of income, attended the synagogue for the traditional service on Fridays and Saturdays, was in good health and had no obvious vices.

Esther said no every time she was presented to such a candidate.

Her parents hinted that it was about time that she became somebody else's responsibility. She was a millstone round their necks, they whispered within her hearing. Now that the boys had left home and no longer needed their shirts washed, starched and ironed every day and her mother no longer needed help with the cooking and household chores, she was no longer needed.

Esther still said no.

She wanted revenge for not being allowed to marry the man she had befriended and later grew to love when she was younger. She was not allowed to marry him, because he had not been chosen by her father in the traditional way. It was not proper for a girl to fall in love. Esther blamed her parents for her disappointment. She blamed herself for not being strong enough to follow her heart. She blamed herself most of all for being too obedient and too down-to-earth, too practical.

She had no means of independent living. That was denied her when her parents withdrew her from school after the baccalaureate and refused to yield to the insistence of her teachers that she should apply for a scholarship for further education. She spent the following years cooking, washing, starching and ironing and also embroidering her dowry. Her school friends married and had children by the time. Esther reached the age of 27, frustrated and still saying no.

The past is sometimes thought of as a perfect golden time. Looking through her late mother's diary, Myra begins to understand her mother's moods, her rages and her longings. Her mother's friendsstill remembred her as a brilliant student, loved by her teachers, yet one of the most rebellious, the leader of their group at school. ..

'Look at Esther, and Marianne, and Jane too,' the girls whispered in the first class after the long summer holiday. 'They've had their hair cut. Very fashionable. A bob – how daring! But wait till the headmistress sees it!'

The school regulations stated that girls should wear their hair long, plaited in braids and hidden under a hair net. But the girls were almost sixteen. During the summer they had spent their time reading all the newspapers and admiring the lovely pictures of fashionable women. This was the first sign of emancipation, of rebellion – the three of them went to the hairdresser.

Myra couldn't stop smiling, proud of her daring mother. After all, this happened in the late 1920s, when rules were strict and children were brought up to obey without flinching.

Sure enough, soon after Assembly, Esther and her friends were summoned to the headmistress's office. Esther went in with her head held high, although she was the smallest of the three, displaying an air of confidence while inside her heart was racing. She had her speech ready; she had rehearsed it in her mind all night.

She had hinted at what was happening over dinner the evening before, but neither Risl, her mother, nor Moshe, her father, seemed interested. Esther's education did not matter to them. She would eventually marry and become a good wife to someone and, being the only girl amongst four brothers, she would have had plenty of practice. Risll would be quite happy to have Esther at home helping in the house.

But Esther had other ideas. She wanted to go to college and become a teacher. The thought of suspension from school, or even being expelled was a terrible prospect and she dreaded it. The thought of staying at home and providing starched white shirts for her brothers every day was depressing her.

The headmistress, a middle-aged, grey-haired woman with her hair in a tight bun, was seated majestically behind her desk on a large carved chair. She looked almost as small and lost in the vastness of the room as the girls in front of her. Yet her eyes flashed with anger.

'Why? Why did you have to? You know what I am asking.' Her questions were aimed mostly at Esther.

She took a deep breath and candidly lifted her blue eyes under her dark eyelashes.

'During the summer we spent a lot of time reading all the newspapers and we could not help admiring Princess Maria. She had her hair cut *"á la garçon"* and we thought if the king's consort did it, we would be allowed to do the same. As a sign of respect for our beloved princess .We read all the books of the beautiful and clever Princess Carmen Sylva as well.' Esther demurely lowered her gaze. 'I am sorry. We all are. We should have asked you first.'

'Quite right. You should have done.'

The girls waited, not daring to breath.

After a pause which seemed to go on for ages, the headmistress said, 'I should expel you. However, because you have done it with the most honourable intentions, you will not be suspended. You are to cover your hair with tight black nets and hide your fringes. This is a warning. This is the last time I will tolerate your misbehaviour.'

'Thank you, thank you,' the girls chorused, their voices sprinkled with tears.

'Off you go now, back to your lessons!'

The three culprits walked backwards out of the office, continuing to murmur their thanks. When they were out of sight and hearing, they hopped and giggled till they fell about.

How proud of them Myra felt. She felt close to her mother and could see herself doing the same.

But all that ended in defeat. Esther could no longer be bothered with the hussle and said yes to Usher.

Her parents were relieved. The brothers put money together and promised to build a house for the young couple in Usher's home town, Barlad, and they paid for the wedding. Perhaps they were happy for her or,were they glad to see the back of her?

Esther went along with these plans, feeling nothing. She and Usher met a few times more. He seemed a nice enough man, quiet, neatly turned out. Still, that did not mean much. He was not rich, not particularly well-connected. He had a small business of his own, but with a widowed mother and an unmarried sister to support he barely made a living.

Still, what could Esther expect? She was nearly 30, long past the age when girls are on the shelf, destined to have become spinsters. She had no means to support herself, she was unable to survive unaided in a male dominated world.

Esther and Usher married in July 1936. She is not smiling in a single picture taken at her wedding. How lucky we are nowadays, Myra thought, and closed the diary.

Esther designed her own wedding dress – that at least was something she could decide for herself. She had the skill and the talent – that was what she was trained for and what she hoped to become, a skilled dressmaker, a specialist artisan. At least now, at her wedding, she could show what she was capable of.

She chose a heavy butter-white silk, which she cut from a pattern she learned at school: a bell-shaped skirt with bell-shaped sleeves. The dress hugged her gentle curves with elegance. She got out the long veil that she had embroidered long before, when she was dreaming of marriage to her David. But that was a dream she had tried hard to dismiss from her mind. There was no point in dwelling on it. Now she was betrothed to Usher, just as her parents wanted, and there was her wedding to get through.

The head-dress, a crown of simple white flowers, was attached to the fine silk of the veil, on which she had embroidered tiny silk birds – birds caught in a net. Did Esther choose this on purpose? It is hard to tell, now she is gone. Her engagement photographs and her wedding photos show her tight-lipped, tense, without the hint of a smile. Perhaps that was what the photographer asked for. Perhaps that was the fashion of the time. Perhaps it showed her fear of what the future might hold.

Usher took his bride to his mother's house in his home town of Barlad further north, in Moldova. Their own house, which was to be built on Usher's land with money given by Esther's four brothers, was not yet ready. She packed her dowry chest with great care, all her memories flooding back as she did so. Her secret letters, written on tiny scraps of paper, she placed at the bottom of the chest. Her clothes patterns, full of happy memories of school along with her dozen complete sets of linen, skilfully embroidered over the years in delicate broderie anglaise, when her thoughts were all of David, who she must now forget. All she had to do now was to add Usher's monogram alongside hers.

She packed all her books. Sometimes, when she felt like it, she would unpack them. The wedding gifts came next: a dinner service from her brother Isaac, a wristwatch encrusted with tiny diamonds from her mother-in-law, and many other gifts from the friends she was leaving behind. On top were all her clothes, made with her own hands, neatly folded and wrapped in tissue paper.

It was a hot day in July 1936 when they arrived in Barlad. The fine dust covering the houses and the trees, and the dirt road increased the feeling of disorder and neglect. The yard with the broken wooden fence without a gate, the small single storey house with a roof showing many broken tiles, kept together with bricks and pieces of wood, the house itself leaning to one side, giving the impression that it would fall down any minute.This was the scene that greeted an already reluctant resident.

4
USHER THE OPTIMIST

Usher was an optimist. He was a man blessed by Fate, and Fortune always smiled on him. He cared nothing for the obstacles in his path – he knew he would overcome them and come through the winner. This deeply-held belief put a smile on his face and a sparkle in his eyes.

At thirty he recently was discharged from the army. He loved the army and he was good at soldiering. Everybody said so, his sergeant and even the captain, who called him in and advised him to change his name to something more Romanian-sounding, so as not to call attention to himself from the regime in charge of the country.

He changed his name by deed poll, but it changed nothing. On his file he was registered: Nationality: Jewish, Religion: Mosaic. So he was out. No more drills and discipline, no more drinking with his mates, no more sport, no more uniform to fascinate the women. He was out. With the tidy sum he had saved, he came home to Anna, his mother, and his sister Clara, now a grown woman.

With time on his hands and no particular skill for civilian life he drifted for a while. His eldest brother Milou, a respectable man, the accountant at the Sharaga Mills, did not offer to find him a job. He thought Usher was still the wild boy he remembered from childhood. From scraps of information Esther got from Anna during the time she stayed at her house, she started to build bit by bit a picture of the man she had married, an insight of his life before they had met.

Usher was the second of four children born to Anna and Adolfo Victor in a small market town near Yashi, the capital of the Moldavia region. The brothers spent their childhood and youth in Barlad, where the family settled. Adolfo, an engineer, was appointed chief mechanic of the town mill. He built a small house with a large garden, and in the following few years Anna bore him two more children.

When the time came to start school Usher, found having to learn things difficult and boring. 'He couldn't be more different from my eldest,' said Anna. Usher was restless and every so often he ran away from school to kick a ball in the fields. He found it hard to learn to read and spell, and having the teachers whack him over his clumsy fingers did not encourage his writing. As for sums, he could not see the need to write them down when he could do them all in his head and come up with the answers before anybody else had put pen to paper. He would blurt out his answers and then switch off, amusing himself by playing with his marbles under the desk. That would lead to another whacking from the teacher. When they got home Milou would waste no time telling Adolfo everything, and that would mean another beating. 'How many times I had to intervene to save Usher. I cannot tell you,' said Anna.

Esther wondered why Anna never lit candles for the Shabbat. She had brought candlesticks from her home and she was determined to stick to tradition, to the way she had been brought up. Then, one day Anna told her a story she remembered:

When Usher was about 12 and Milou a year older, Adolfo hired an old rabbi to teach the boys the prayers and the Hebrew alphabet in preparation for their bar mitzvah, when a Jewish boy becomes a man. The ever-clever and studious Milou excelled. He learned the alphabet and the prayers, while Usher spent his time observing the old man in his shiny black caftan, with his long white beard, and listening to the way he was chanting the prayers. When the rabbi's eyes closed as sleep overtook him, Usher would slip out for 'a breath of fresh air.' He would come back after a while and sit down quietly before the old man noticed anything amiss. The Hebrew lessons took place after school and as the evening advanced, they continued by the light of candles. Usher became interested at how soft hot wax was, and how it attached itself to surfaces. He thought it would be a good idea to experiment with the rabbi's beard. As the old man's head sank forward, overtaken by the weight of old age and sleep, Usher deftly applied soft wax to the rabbi's beard. That was the end of Usher's religious education.

Another punishment followed, and another, and Usher finally ran away from home. He stowed away on a train which took him to Galatzi, the big town and harbour on the Danube. He drifted for a while until he found a clock and watch maker who took him on as an apprentice.

He was happy there and loved the work; he soon learned how clocks worked, and he made himself useful running errands. The watchmaker loved him like his own son and praised him. Usher felt that Fate was smiling on him.

That good life did not last long. Adolfo found him and took him back. At home Anna had her hands full with a new baby boy. The following year she gave birth to a baby girl. Not long after, Adolfo died. It was tetanus, and his death was very sudden so he did not have to suffer a long and horrible illness. 'I stopped saying prayers after that,' said Anna.

The mill owners considered their duty and paid for Milou to enter the Commercial Secondary School. There was no aid for Anna and her younger children. Usher registered as a cadet in the Army. He was fourteen years old and he felt he had fallen on his feet. Life was smiling on him again.

But now so many years later, here he was back home again, with Anna, who was skin and bones, bent over by constant sewing, her eyesight failing, and Goutzu, who had learned his trade as an Army conscript. Little Clara was now grown up with a position as apprentice to a seamstress.

Usher found an old Army mate whose father had a small timber yard. The man wanted to retire and Usher bought him out. That was a new beginning. That was something he could do – run his own business. There was a little money left over and with it he bought a piece of land where he planned to build a house of his own. He did not find civilian life easy. There was a lot of planning to do, the kind of decisions he did not have to worry about as a soldier. As soon as he started to earn he helped his mother and sister a little.

He made a good job of managing the timber yard. He knew his beams and plywood and his hardwood from his softwood logs. He could tell the position of each as soon as he walked into the yard. He could advise his clients, calculating in his head the exact quantities they needed to build a house. He did not need pen and paper except when ordering stock, and then he went to ask Milou for help.

Anna started nagging him: 'Why don't you get married? Why don't you settle down? Look at you. A strong handsome lad should have a home of his own and children.'

Usher did not want to be tied down just yet. He knew he was good looking, with his wavy black hair, brown eyes and clear complexion. He was not very tall, but with his upright army bearing and bulging muscles, he cut quite a dash. 'Shut up mother. One thing at a time'. he would say, peppering his speech with a few swearwords, familiar from his time in the army. But Usher usually listened and in the end did what his mother said. He was getting fed up with his life at home, his younger brother in the state he was, his mother and sister forever busy with their sewing, his income never enough to cover all their needs. He realised that he was also lonely. Years away had made him a stranger in his home town. His school pals had all taken different paths and dispersed. So he discussed marriage with his elder brother, the wise one, the settled one, and the decision was taken: Usher would get married.

He did not know many nice girls. The girls he did know were not the marrying kind. They were great fun, but not the sort his mother would approve of. So he contacted a matchmaker, who introduced him to some nice girls from good families. One after another he visited them in the presence of his brother and the girls' relations. Some were pretty but too pale. Some wore too much makeup. The parents of others looked at him with suspicion when they realised there was not much money involved.

The matchmaker finally advised him to go and visit a respectable God-fearing family. The girl, Esther, had four well-off brothers who were prepared to help. Usher took the train to Focshani, a town 300 kilometres south of his home. His brother Milou came with him for support.

Esther, a little woman with fierce blue eyes and pursed lips, stirred some interest in him. She said yes to his proposal. He liked that. He felt she was a challenge. He visited Esther several more times and he was really taken by her looks, her proud demeanour, the way she looked at him fearlessly, straight in the eyes, the elegant way she wore her clothes. He felt a little in awe of her, but he told himself that once they were married, he could teach her a thing or two. They became engaged, and she allowed him to kiss her. Usher felt good. Life had started to smile on him yet again.

They were married in July. It was a lavish wedding and Usher felt like a million dollars, dressed in top hat and tails, with this elegant, grave, unsmiling woman at his side. He brought his new wife to his home town and they moved into their new house as soon as it was ready. Money was tight but they managed. All Usher asked of Esther was that she cook and clean and give him his manly due. Esther found this hard to adjust to. She had hoped for some conversation, some meeting of minds, some gentleness in intimate relations, but it was not to be. And Usher was jealous. She could not use make-up or lipstick. She could not even express a liking for a movie star, or an argument would start. 'What do you find in him I haven't got?' It was impossible to reason with Usher. In those days a woman had to put up with it all. There was nowhere she could go. She could neither live alone nor go back to her parents.

Esther was sitting outside in the yard at Anna's. Their house was not ready. It was a lovely afternoon, the sun still up in the sky, the shadows longer and the leaves flying in the dusty wind a reminder of the coming winter. She had a book on her lap but could not concentrate on reading. She was listening to broken fragments of conversation which reached her from inside the house through the open windows. Usher had come back from work and gone to see his mother. Esther thought they were talking about her...or was she getting paranoid? Anna was saying something about lonely and understandable.

'Hey Esther, put that book away, you will ruin your eyes!'

Esther pretended she had not heard him .She abandoned the book and stared into space. In the distance 's shape by the river stood immobile like a statue. Long shadows stretched across the river. Through the window single words like seeds thrown at random: Sullen ..understandable lonely...uppity... ran back and forth hitting her ears Yes, Esther was thinking, she had a lot to learn: how to laugh at silly, sometimes coarse jokes, how to please him in bed, how to smile more often...

Usher felt once they were in their own home things would settle. He had already started to listen to his wife and take note of her wishes. He thought they were a lucky couple. But, Usher had always been an optimist.

5
ANNA

Anna was widowed early. She never could understand how a tiny cut on her husband's hand led to such a horrible death. With a permanent smile and locked jaws Anna's Adolfo had gone, leaving her with four children to raise by herself.

Anna was not from those parts. Her family were peasants way up in the mountains, so she had no one to help her. The children ran wild. It was a miracle, Anna said, that they had turned out quite well, what with Usher in the army, Milou a qualified accountant and Clara beginning to get work as a seamstress, her only worry remained her second son, Gutzu. It was such a pity that he was the way he was, but he was harmless, she reassured Esther. Esther was surprised that Usher had never mentioned he had another brother. It made her even more uneasy about the marriage.

Later, in their tiny room, Usher told her what had happened to Gutzu. He was the first of the brothers to marry his sweetheart. He had his own little business and built his house on the river bank all by himself. Then there was heavy rain which went on for weeks. The River Tutova burst its banks and flooded the land, taking with it all that stood in its way: the trees, the animals, the people. Anna's house was damaged but survived. 's house was swept away. Among the dead were Gutzu's wife and his unborn child. From that day, more than three years ago, had never spoken a word to anyone. He just sat there, where his home

28

once stood, winter and summer. All attempts to approach him were greeted with aggression, so they let him be. There was no point in talking about him, Usher said. There was nothing to say. 'But I wonder what my parents and my brothers would have said if they had known', Esther thought.

That was how the young couple started their new life together. It was not an ideal match, but that was the way it was, for better or worse, whichever came first. Newlyweds had to bury their disappointment and resentment and give it a go. Things would get better. Perhaps.

When the pain and depression of a difficult birth were passed, Esther finally got her reward: her little girl. She planned to teach her, to encourage her to study and achieve everything she had been prevented from doing in her life. Myra grew quickly, she walked and talked early. Esther kept a weekly count in her diary of how many new words Myra learned.

'On your second birthday you knew two hundred words and could recite a nursery rhyme and everyone applauded!' she told Myra with pride. It cheered an otherwise dull day.

6
MEMORIES

Myra could not say when the world around her became significant enough to have left such a deep trace on her memory. The earliest times she remembered were of the long days spent in the kitchen at the bottom of the garden, where the iron stove was constantly burning and her mamma cooked tasty dishes, ironed clothes with an iron full of burning charcoal, dressed her and made ringlets of her hair with the hot iron tongs. It hurt but Myra was not allowed to cry. The people who lived at the front of the house might hear her. Daddy came back in the evening and Mama lay the table in the one room, which served as dining room, bedroom and playroom. She carried the dinner in from the kitchen.At night Myra slept in her cot, which had shiny bars and angels painted on the white panels. It sat under the window and Mama and Daddy had their divan bed propped against the opposite wall. The room opened onto a tiny hall where there was a hatch over the entrance to the cellar and a door leading outside and to the kitchen.

Myra wondered why they all had to live in that back room if it was her parents' house. And why was she not allowed to play by the front gate?

As soon as she was able to understand, Mama told her that in September 1939 the Germans had invaded Poland, and Britain and France declared war on Germany. Romania drifted towards and became allied with Germany and the black shirts caused mischief everywhere, especially for the Jews. In time, the persecution of Jews became increasingly severe. Things got worse. The house that Myra's parents had built together and cherished, was requisitioned by the Romanian army and the family were confined to one room at the back of the house and the kitchen. An important military man and his wife were housed in the best part of the house. That was why Myra had to be quiet and not disturb those people, and that was why she was stopped from making the front gate squeak when she climbed on its ledge and moved it to and fro. Myra's memory of the war, beside falling bombs, was the noise and the fear and the constant reminders to be quiet. Quiet because the grown-ups were upset, quiet so they could hear the sirens sounding their threatening wail. Quiet so that they could hear Aunt Rosa's high heeled shoes making a hurried noise: tik, tok, tik, tock on the plank leading to the shelter. Quiet not to draw attention to themselves; 'there are enemies living in our own house!'

1942. The day started quietly. Esther washed and dressed Myra and the fearful iron curlers went on the stove to set Myra's hair. At the same time Esther was listening intently to the noises from the sky. Next door, Aunt Rosa was peelings tomatoes and onions which Mr Istrick, her husband, had brought in fresh from the garden. Aunt Rosa was going to make a large salad and Myra couldn't wait because she knew she would be invited to join the feast. Esther curled Myra's hair in ringlets. Myra was in tears because the attention to her hair was, as usual, painful . Esther asked her to hold up her two index fingers, to which she attached a white ribbon, which she folded and knotted in the middle in the shape of a butterfly. It was going to be put in Myra's hair.

Then suddenly she became aware of Aunt Rosa's high heels on the march towards the shelter. Within seconds the sirens began to scream and distant roaring sounds signalled the approach of the bombardment. There was just enough time to pour water over the fire, then Esther and Myra ran through the little side gate into the Istricks' garden to the shelter

The shelter was a primitive dwelling, just a deep hole in the ground, large enough to hold twenty people, covered with a canvas on which the residents had laid thick tree branches to hide it from view. Afew benches were set inside for people to sit on. Wooden ladders were propped up at the two entrances to allow people to come in and out. As the sky filled with the deafening sound of aeroplanes and the air filled with smoke, Esther and Myra just made it to the shelter. Mr Istrick caught Myra and Esther followed down the ladder. In the shelter there was no room to sit on the bench so they sat on the earth floor. Esther, breathless and shivering, held Myra's hand so tight it hurt, but the child's protests went unheard.

The noise was so low, so close, that the planes might be hovering just above their heads. All the people in the shelter curled up into balls, covering their ears with their hands. The noise eased bit by bit. No bombs had been heard falling nearby. A few women lifted their heads and started making the sign of the cross. Then the plane returned, and sounded as if, again, it was hovering just above them.

Myra wet herself. Aunt Rosa made funny noises that sounded like crying. Julius, her son, had recently started smoking a pipe and Myra noticed that the pipe shook and clattered between his teeth. She would have thought it was funny, if she hadn't been so worried about what her mother would say about her wet pants.

The air raid was over at last, but the people in the shelter waited patiently for the siren to sound the all clear. Even when the danger was over some people were sick. There was a heavy smell of fuel, sweat and sick. They waited a while until they felt sure the planes were not coming back, then fearfully climbed out one by one. There was no bomb damage this time, but in the yards, the fields, all around them, there were millions of leaflets. Among the leaflets were toys, miniature cars, pens, little balls. Myra started running to grab a toy but Esther shouted: 'Don't touch! They could be poisoned'. Myra could not read what was written on the small pieces of paper and her mum, having read them, screwed them up and threw them into the fire she had just rekindled.

Myra hovered uncertainly near her mother and finally plucked up enough courage to own up to wetting herself. Mother was angry, so angry. Myra was frightened. She wished Daddy would come home soon. Even Fanny next door came running, having heard the shouts. Esther was screaming and crying about this horrible life. In her distress she was cursing her fate that had lumbered her with this kid to have to take care of. 'And look, Fanny, what she has done, after months of training!' Esther had to cope with this all by herself. Myra meantime did not dare to cry and tried to make herself invisible. Then things settled down – until the next time. By the time Daddy came home all was quiet and Myra said nothing in case they started arguing, and that would be, again, her fault.

'Go and see your grandma Anna,' Esther told Myra. 'See if they are all right.' By now Myra was cleaned and changed. She was pleased her mother was talking to her again. It meant she was forgiven. The cobbled street was still littered with leaflets from Myra's house to Grandma's. There was no one to see her, so Myra picked one up, but she could not read. The little toys were inviting as they rolled to and fro in the wind but she was too scared to touch. Mamma said they were full of poison specially sent by the Germans to kill children.

Another way to Grandma's lay through the churchyard, which had been empty and neglected since the priest and his family left. There were wild flowers and long grasses, and little yellow and white camomile flowers to pick. At Grandma's all was well. Both Anna and Clara were hard at work at their sewing as if nothing had happened. Myra stayed chatting with them for a while. She watched as Grandma stitched a hem and Clara dressed a mannequin in some cloth she put together in the shape of a blouse and with deft fingers cut round the neckline and arm holes.

'Better go home now, darling,' said Anna, 'in case we have another bombardment and your mother and father would worry so.'

Myra hesitated to go out because she would have to pass in front of Gutzu and she was scared of him. Gingerly she squeezed past him. He never moved. She ran all the way home still holding the little bunch of wild flowers she had gathered.

Days passed, one after another, following the same routine. Esther stuck thin strips of paper criss-cross on the windows to prevent flying glass. She bought sheaves of black paper and lined the outside windows, which she closed as soon as night fell and the blackout began.

7
DADDY WENT AWAY

Myra did not cry when her Daddy, Usher went away. She did not know if she would not upset him with her crying. She did not understand exactly that he would be away such a long time. But Esther cried and Myra felt sad without understanding why. After he left, Esther explained that he had gone with other Jewish men to the work camps by the order of General Antonescou. The men were sent to Northern Moldavia and then to the Ukraine. That was far away and Daddy would not come back soon. Myra was relieved to hear that it was not Mama's fault, nor because of the accident...

Daddy went away just a few weeks after the accident. Usher came home late that night, after yet another row with Esther. Myra lay in bed awake and frightened and silent. She was waiting for her Daddy and she felt glad when she heard the little gate squeaking and heavy steps passing He entered the house through the kitchen door and made his way to the bedroom in the dark, passing through the little front hall. In the hall the hatch doors to the cellar, lay open. They were normally very careful to keep the hatch shut, but that night, when Esther went down to fetch wood, she was so upset after the row that she forgot. Usher, creeping along in the dark so as not to wake Myra, stepped right into the black hole.

'Esther,' he howled, his voice full of pain 'Get someone.! I'm hurt.'

'Oh, dear God,' she said. 'I forgot. Oh dear, oh dear,' she lamented. 'Stay there. I will go and fetch help.' She put on her coat and walked down the street to where the doctor lived. 'Oh dear,' she said. 'Now he will say I did it on purpose.' On her way back she knocked at the Istricks' next door and asked them to help.

Usher had a broken arm, which was put in a plaster cast. Esther kept saying she was sorry and it had been an accident but, as she predicted, he did not believe her and kept repeating: 'You'd like to see me dead, wouldn't you.?'

Myra did not understand. Her Mama was crying every day and Daddy was in pain from his broken arm. Myra was so sorry for him. If he had to leave, she feared that she would be left alone. She could not sleep .She would have liked to cry but she did not dare.

Soon the tension and recriminations of her parents were cut short, and other worries took over. At the end of 1942, a letter came from the police commandant, ordering Usher to present himself at the town hall for mobilisation. Most Jewish men were mobilised in the same way. They were to wear their coats with the yellow star visible on their breast pocket. Esther and Usher began to make plans in the face of this new disaster. First, Usher decided to sell Esther's bracelet watch and other pieces of jewellery to leave her with some money, in case they took him away. Both parents sat Myra down and swore her to secrecy – after all, the watch was a wedding gift from Grandma Anna. Then he paid a visit to his

37

brother Milou. Milou did not get the dreaded letter, he was not called away. He was too useful to the town. He gave Usher some money and asked him to leave in case he drew the authorities' attention to him as well.

A few days later, Usher had a bright idea : 'Esther, where did you put the plaster cast?' Esther looked at him but said nothing. There was no point in saying anything. Once he had an idea in his head, no matter how foolish, he would not change. He hoped that if he showed his plaster cast, worn over the sleeve of his coat so it would be visible, he would not be taken. He will plead not fit for work. But it did not sway the doctor or the police official.   Some Jewish men stayed behind – those who had money, and those who were considered important to the normal functioning of the town, like Milou, who was essential to the working of the mill – but Usher was not one of them. Esther packed his bag with warm clothes, toiletries, pen and paper. He kissed Esther goodbye, gave Myra a long hug and off he went.

There was less food to eat because money from Esther's brothers stopped coming by post. The neighbours helped as much as they could, but life was hard. By late 1943 the raids became very frequent, and most nights were disrupted by the sirens and the race to the underground shelter. In between times they were waiting anxiously for the next raid.

Esther started to teach Myra to read from the old primary school book someone gave her as a present. It kept them both occupied. Surica, another neighbour, gave Myra a present for her birthday a slate and white chalk, so Myra started to learn the alphabet. Esther knitted a grey pullover with long sleeves for Usher, hoping that she could send it to him at his new location. Letters from him came once in a while from different places, months after they were written, so there was never any certainty about his address.

In the autumn of 43, the Romanian officer and his wife left the house. He was posted to the front. A group of German soldiers with their commandant took their place and moved in.

8
THE GARDEN

Myra sat on her chair by the kitchen window while Mama combed her hair. She looked longingly at the stretch of land in front of her eyes. This was her garden. There were no flowers in her garden, nor any trees. No benches either. It was a narrow stretch of cobblestones extending from the kitchen, along the side of the house to the front gate. The cobbles hurt her tender feet, but it was Myra's garden. On its way to the road in front of the house, the garden passed in front of the winter kitchen, which was no longer a kitchen but a bedroom shared with Myra's Mama. Myra's bed was by the window. The best thing was that, being near her Mama, she did not have to fear a thing. Second best was that on her bed she could stand up and stretch her neck so she could see, above the bars of her cot and over the window sill, her beloved garden.

She knew each stone she could see and gave them names, according to the colours that she had recently learned. There were brown stones like the earth, red stones like the roof of the house and grey stones, the colour of the aeroplanes that zoomed overhead. The grey ones were spiky, the brown ones were rounded and gentle, and so were the sand-coloured ones. The red ones were flat and square and best to hop on barefoot. They formed zig-zag and diamond patterns.

When Mama stuck a criss-cross of thin tapes across the window to stop the glass shattering in a bomb blast, Myra was vexed at first, but after a while she found a new game. She divided the stones into the triangles of light that filtered through the gaps, and she could see and count the stones fitting into each frame. It was her game to choose how many red, or sand or grey or speckled stones came into each frame, depending where she stood on the bed.

The cobbled garden did not know of Myra's games. Unconcerned, it followed its path past the rear entrance steps that led to the cellar. That was the cellar where Daddy fell one night and broke his arm, because Mama forgot to close the hatch. That was before they took Daddy away to the camp. Perhaps his arm got better, Myra thought.

Beyond the rear entrance the garden narrowed further, to make room for the larger part of the house. This was the garden Myra did not know. She was not allowed beyond that point because soldiers lived there, soldiers in green uniforms who did not know that the family who lived in the tiny rooms at the rear of the house were Jews. Mama said that if they knew who Myra was there would be no more play, no house, and the cobbled garden would have new masters. The soldiers wore black shiny boots which made a loud crunchy noise on the cobbles.

That summer Myra learned to hop. She hopped from the kitchen door to the rear porch. She chose to hop on the red stones, following the pattern. Not because they were red, but because they were flatter and there were fewer of them. She often fell, but cried silently. She knew the rules. She knew the green-uniformed men with shiny black boots and the strange cross on their lapels were German soldiers. She could hear them sometimes, singing and talking in a language she could not understand. In the evenings Myra said goodbye to her garden and the stones as blackness descended beyond the criss-crossed windows. Myra wondered if the stones slept or cried under the weight of the heavy black boots.

In the mornings, when Mama was cooking and the sirens were not spreading the sound of approaching danger, Myra would be out playing and, little by little, inch by inch, she extended the size of her territory, hoping Mama would not notice.

A little further, a little further, just to see the colour of the other stones, or if grass grew between the stones. Nobody noticed. Mama was chatting to the neighbours. Myra ran back before anyone could notice where she had been.

The next day she went a little further. New cobbled stones, a new game, new feelings, the thrill of danger, of exploring and being daring. She wanted to see when Mama would begin to notice.

One day she reached the main door of the house. The door was wide open. Foreign voices came from inside. Panic engulfed her and she ran back to safety as fast as she could.

Still nobody noticed. Mama was too busy that day chatting with Julian, who lived next door. She often spoke and laughed with Julian. She was being naughty too, Myra thought. Before he left

Daddy told Mama not to chat with that young man. He had been idle since he was thrown out of university, where Jewish people were no longer allowed to study. Nor had he been taken to the camp, because he was rich and had managed to get out of it. But Mama always liked to chat with Julian, just as she did that day, leaning against the little gate between the two gardens.

The next day was a hot summer day, stifling hot. Mama let Myra out early. She was very busy. She had to finish her chores before the expected bombing raid. Myra did not wait to be told twice. She checked and talked to each row of stones. She jumped on some, stood on tip-toe on others, knelt down to pat the top of a few. Slowly she moved forward, row after row, past the door to the cellar, past the edge of the wider rooms, slowly forward to the main entrance of the house.

All of a sudden she became aware of a pair of shiny boots. She froze. She screwed her eyes tight and stood rooted to the spot. After a while she opened her eyes just a little. The boots had not moved. Nor had they crushed her. She shut her eyes again, and opened them again.

She lifted her gaze along the green trousers with a band down the side, climbing upwards as she raised her eyes. She took in the shiny buttons of his tunic, the rifle held in a hairy hand sticking out of a sleeve with a black-on-white-on-black funny cross. She shut her eyes tight again.

'*Ein kind! Hello.*' She heard the voice from above. She did not move.

After what seemed like ages she heard some paper rustling. Was he going to kill her? She wanted to call 'Mama', but no sound came out.

The rustling continued. Myra turned her head towards the kitchen. There was no sign of Mama, from where she was standing. She was lost.

Then a pair of green knees appeared .The boots squeaked as the knees came down lower and lower, until they were at her eye level. A hand appeared holding a thin brown square, half covered in shiny paper. The hand lowered to reach her face.

'Bite. *Eat. Ess.*'

Myra kept her eyes and her lips shut. The brown square touched her lips and chin. It smelt good. Instinctively she licked her lips. It tasted good. She took a bite of the brown square and licked her lips again.

'More,' the voice said. It was good. The hand rested on the green trousers on the bent knee.

'Once more.' Myra ate it all.

The voice began to laugh. The knees straightened and so did the boots. Then they turned and walked away.

Myra stayed for a few seconds on the cobbled stones, then with all her strength she ran like the wind back to her Mama. She found her seated on a stool, at work on the grey sweater she was knitting for Daddy. She lifted her eyes and saw Myra.

'What's that round your mouth. Come near. Where did you get chocolate from?'

A thought suddenly dawned on Mama. Two burning slaps hit Myra's cheeks.

9
THE REFUGEES

Rumours started to circulate that the war had taken a turn. In the shelters people were saying that the Russians were gaining ground. The bombardments intensified. The town, which happened to be at the cross-roads, was being bombed twice: by the Germans as they advanced into Russia and again when they returned being chased by the Russians. In 1943 the American planes joined in the fun.

A new fear was that Romania would be carved in two. Moldavia, just north of Focsani, where the border between Moldavia and Valachia lay, would be taken by the Russians. Esther was beside herself with worry. If this happened it would mean she would not have a husband and she would be separated from her parents and brothers for ever. They would be on the north side of the order with the Russians.

How could a child three years old, nearly four, remember dates and times? All Myra could recall was that the snow vanished leaving in its wake big puddles and mushy mud. In the neglected churchyard across the road snowdrops and crocuses started showing their heads, and on the ground a carpet of bright green appeared, covering the dead twigs and leaves, wiping out any memory of the previous autumn and winter.

The swallows appeared in tight symmetrical formations, oblivious of the air raids, even though many died or disappeared because of them. The storks came back and set up home in the belfry of the Church and on the highest chimneys; the few that were still standing. Sharp blizzards and frosts, changing speedily into rain, still came, on and off. Esther said they were called 'baba', because they were like moody and grumpy old women. The nights were still very cold.

It was at this time, one morning in the early spring of 1944, that Myra woke up to see her mother packing. All their belongings went into the divan bed, which opened to reveal a large storage space. Esther filled the space with clothes, bedding, pots, cutlery. In went Myra's books and Esther's books, including her beloved *Gone With The Wind*. In went letters, toys, even the rag doll Esther had made, together with the rag ball. Surprised, Myra started asking questions.

'Where are we going, Mama? Am I coming too?'

'Of course you are coming,' Esther said, going on with her packing. 'Just don't ask any questions. I will tell you later.'

'But how are we going to carry this?' Where are we going?'

'Don't worry, there will be a nice man who will come with a horse and a wagon and take us far away. It will be an adventure.'

'Who is this man, Mama?'

'He is a friend of Uncle Leon, who lives in Bucharest. He has asked this friend of his who is a policeman, to help us. Don't worry, he is not a bad policeman! This is a big secret and you must not tell anyone. You hear me? If you do, I'll leave you behind, all by yourself.'

Sirens stared to sound, warning of danger approaching. Aunt Rosa's red high heels started their march to the shelter. The soldiers billeted in the front of the house emerged running and boarded an army lorry.

'Remember, not a word to Fanny or Rosa,' Esther repeated. Myra nodded in obedience.

Bombs fell nearby. The noise and dust from the precarious ceiling covered the inmates of the shelter. They could hear glass breaking and wondered what they would find above ground when the raid was over. If they should come out alive. Anti-aircraft guns sounded in repetitive short bursts. Then a loud explosion shook the shelter, so near that people started running to the opposite exit, pushing to be first to climb the ladder and escape.

The bomb left a great hole in the street just in front of the house. All the windows were shattered and the front doors lay on the ground in broken bits of wood . Esther did not dare to approach the front rooms, which now stood derelict, in case the German soldiers came back and found her trespassing.

'Just as well we are leaving soon,' Esther whispered. 'So long as nothing else happens.'

A cold wind was blowing through the empty windows and there was nothing to light a fire with, so Esther and Myra huddled together under a blanket. They ate a cold meal of leftover polenta and some butter.

Later a man came to the house. He was of middle years, a thin, dark man with a moustache. His name was Loupou. Silver teeth sparkled when he smiled. He was Uncle Leon's friend and, as arranged, he said that just after it got dark, he would come with a wagon. He asked Esther to cover her head with a shawl, in the manner of a Romanian peasant, and to get Myra to do the same and be ready; they could not linger in case someone noticed. The German soldiers were gone, so they could get away a little easier. They would pretend Esther was his sister, and Myra had to call him uncle. He had booked a room for the night at an inn near the Siret, the great river that separates Walachia from runs through Moldavia in its way to the the Danube. In the early hours of the next morning they would cross the river. There was a horse drawn ferry that was still working, taking people across.

'Are we saying goodbye to Grandma and Clara and Uncle Milou?' Myra asked.

'Not now. We'll write to them later, You keep quiet!' Esther replied.

It was so cold Myra started shivering. Esther made some tea on the primus stove, but Myra could not drink it. Her throat was sore.

Evening came, and the wagon was loaded with the bed that held all their possessions. Uncle Loupou and Esther climbed onto the seat beside the driver, an old man with a thick moustache who coughed a thick cough. Myra was sat comfortably at the back amidst the luggage and she did not protest. She felt listless and hot.

Without a word to anyone, and in the hope that no one noticed their departure, they left.

Myra did not say goodbye to her grandma, but by the time they left she felt so ill that the thought did not cross her mind again. She felt hot and cold at the same time, and her throat hurt and her eyes felt sore.

They took a road through the woods that was full of holes and bumps. They had to stop a couple of times for Myra to be sick. They were hoping to avoid drawing attention to themselves and to avoid any air raids and Uncle Loupou was getting impatient. They were stopped once by a patrol, at the outskirts of the town, and Uncle Loupou presented his papers. He was a policeman and he was wearing his uniform. He said he was taking his sister and niece to visit their elderly parents, and they were allowed to pass without further questions.

When they reached the inn it was dark, the sun long gone, and Myra felt so hot her Mama was beside herself with worry. But Esther knew that whatever happened there was nothing she could do. There was no way back.

At the inn Esther asked for some water, took it to her room and sponged Myra, who by then was hallucinating. Uncle Loupou went down to have a drink and something to eat. He brought up food for Esther. By then Myra was covered in spots and whimpered in a restless sleep.

'What are we going to do?' Esther asked, crying.   'We will not be allowed on the ferry!'

'There's nothing we can do. We must go on. There is no way we can tell anyone she has what looks like scarlet fever. We can only hope that if she stays with us and we cover her up it will not spread to others.'

Myra woke up feeling groggy and miserable. She opened her eyes. It was dark outside and she could hear water splashing rhythmically.

'Mamma,' she cried weakly, not finding her voice.

'Sssh, keep quiet,' she heard her mother saying.

'I'm thirsty.'

'Keep quiet. I'll give you a drink.'

'Where are we?'

'We are crossing the river on the ferry. We covered you with straw, so don't worry if you get straw in your mouth. Soon we shall be safe.'

There were other people on the ferry. Myra could hear them, talking quietly. All refugees. There were horses and wagons too. Then she fell asleep.

When she woke again it was daylight and the sun was shining brightly. The wagon was passing through a town with a broad street. Myra opened her eyes with difficulty as they seemed stuck together. Her hands were red and her palms were peeling. Her throat was sore and she had no voice.

The wagon stopped in front of a large gate with iron palings pointing to the sky. Beyond the gate, in the distance, there was a large house screened by rose bushes. Through her sticky eyes Myra could barely distinguish the elderly woman, not too tall, with greying red hair gathered in a bun, a

51

shawl round her shoulders and an apron over her dark-coloured dress, who came out to greet them. Behind her came a tall, dark, elderly man wearing a grey country hat.

'Come, Myra. Say hello to your granny and grandpa,' said Esther. 'Mother, she was ill all the way, it was a nightmare. Perhaps you should not touch her as she is ill.' She pointed to Myra's spots and flushed face.

'Never mind. Come in,' said the elderly man. 'Thank you, Mr Loupou, for bringing them. Come in. Let's not draw attention to ourselves. Come in and have a drink.'

It was a large house with high ceilinged rooms, larger even than the house where Aunt Rosa and Mr Istrick lived. Myra was put to bed after her mother had given her a large drink and forced her to drink, then washed off all the dirt and grime of the journey. Grandma helped her undress. Myra whimpered in pain; all movement made her body hurt.

Myra was miserable and frightened. Grandma was not smiling. In fact she looked a little menacing, with her right eye slightly closed and squinting. Later Myra understood that she could not speak Romanian. She only spoke Yiddish, mostly to give orders.

In the morning, the fever abated and Myra woke up feeling a little better. She could hear Esther talking to her father.

'Perhaps we should call the doctor, in case she has complications.'

'Not possible, Esther. Nobody will come here. Nobody in this neighbourhood knows who we are. We don't want to draw attention to ourselves. And we are just in front of the German Command centre here. Look, across the road. See?'

'As you say, Father. Let's just pray she will get through this.'

Myra made a good recovery, with no complications. Later on she thought how tough she must have been, to have recovered with no medicines to help. It must be because Grandpa prayed so hard. She had never seen anyone pray like that before.

As soon as she was back on her feet Myra started to investigate this large house. There was a large kitchen with shiny copper pans hanging on a rack above the large kitchen range. In the middle of the room there was a heavy wooden table with chairs. There was a cold storage room where flour, maize and beans were stored. She had never seen so much flour in sacks before.

At the back of the house there was a scullery and a toilet with a proper seat made of wood, and water that came from a tap. There was a shed at the back of the garden where grandpa kept his working tools. Such a lot of things to explore!

The front entrance was locked and had its shutters closed. Nobody was allowed to enter there. The curtains were drawn and Myra could not see inside. Just like their house in Barlad, only no Germans seemed to live there. In the large garden the plum tree bore white flowers and the cherry tree was in bud.

Grandpa was working in the garden. Myra stood and watched how he parted the soil into straight rows and marked the rows with wooden twigs and drew a string between the twigs. Then he sowed little seeds in each row. In one of the rows, he dug holes at even distances and started putting in green tiny plants.

After a while Grandpa looked up and smiled.

'Come and help me,' he said. Myra came willingly

That is how she learned the green leaves were tomatoes plants, which by the late summer would bear juicy red tomatoes. The seeds were beans and peas. Her job was to pour a little water into the hole before and after Grandpa planted something. They became good pals, although he did not talk much.

It was harder with Grandma, who spoke only Yiddish with Esther so Myra could not understand. In time Myra picked up some Yiddish, and Grandma taught her the morning prayer: *Mode any leffu nechu shechu zartu.* It did not mean a thing to Myra, but she was pleased that it made her Mama and Grandma happy.

Summer was approaching. The rose buds were bursting into bloom and the scent was overwhelming. Esther came out each morning and cut fresh flowers which she put in water in the room that she shared with her daughter.

Myra was happy. Here they did not have to go to the shelter and although the sirens sounded from time to time, only distant planes could be heard. She started to understand Grandma but she did not tell any of them, so she could listen in to what had been said..

'Mama,' she asked, 'are Grandma and Grandpa very rich? They have such a lovely house.'

'No darling. Grandpa is not rich. He is no longer working and this is not their house.'

'Whose house is it then?'

'It belongs to a very rich family, friends of Uncle Leon. The man was called up to fight in the war, and his wife and daughter left for the country, in a village up in the mountains, away from the bombs and where there is plenty of food. Uncle Leon feared that grandma and grandpa would be picked up and be taken to a camp, like so many Jewish people. On their street, everybody knew them so it was not safe. It was better for them to move somewhere where nobody knew them. Uncle Leon's friend was only too eager to leave his house and his belongings in safe keeping, so it was arranged. Grandma and Grandpa would live here until the war was over.'

'Ah, that is why the front rooms are locked,' said Myra.

'Don't you dare go there, or you will get another slap!

The house was just opposite the German headquarters and Myra, when Mama was busy elsewhere, spent a lot of time hidden in the rose bushes watching. Soldiers in green uniforms came and went. Twice a day they were marched down the street in tight rows and an officer kept them in step, calling *eintz, zwei, drei,* or *links, recht, links* , the soldiers sometimes lifting their legs as high as they could. When the marching finished they would salute and say 'Heil Hitler!'

Myra had a secret. It was not of her doing, it just happened. The German soldiers had a dog, a very large woolf like dog. Mama said it was called a German shepherd. He walked every day with one of the soldiers, even marched in step with them, keeping his place. The soldiers called him Lux and he responded to his name.

When Myra told Esther of her discovery she got another slap and Esther told her in a stern voice never to call the dog, and when it appeared she must run indoors. Myra never called him, but stayed watching Lux from behind the bushes.

One day while the soldier kept guard by the great door, the dog looked in her direction, tugged at its lead and pulled the soldier towards her. Myra's heart beat fast in her chest and she was rooted to the spot. Lux did not bark, just sniffed. The soldier looked down and spotted Myra. A broad smile appeared on his face. He said some words and took something from his pocket. Myra thought he was about to kill her. Instead he held out a small shiny packet of chocolate and gave it to her. It was like what had happened before in her garden. Myra did not thank him: she had lost the power of speech. When she recovered from her shock, she guzzled down the chocolate and hid the paper. Then she went and had a drink and washed her face with water from the garden tap It took a day or two before she dared hide in the bushes and look through the fence again. When she did, the same thing happened. She never told her mother. She kept this secret for ever.

All too soon, threatening clouds gathered again.

Myra did not understand why one day a few policemen came and ordered Myra and her mother to return to the town where they came from because they had no right to leave without permission. They had noticed Esther was absent from her cleaning duties at the Police station where Jewish women had to sign in once a week. Myra and Esther were ordered to return under police guard. Grandma and Grandpa were spoken to in harsh terms by the Romanian policeman. Esther hurried to pack a small suitcase and they left immediately. They were taken to the train station and travelled all the way back accompanied by one of the policemen.

He was nice, and kept saying, 'Not to worry, it is the law. If you ask for permission and fill the forms, you could come back.'

Esther asked him if it was possible to enter her street and house without him so that the neighbours would not think she was being brought back like a prisoner. He said, 'Of course,' and advised her to come to the police station the next day and fill in the forms, officially applying to go to live with her parents. He reassured her that she will be successful.

They entered the empty house. The whole house was deserted. The front windows were gone and a door was squeaking to and fro in the breeze. The German occupants who left some time ago never returned. Aunt Rosa and Fanny were not there to greet them. Mama said, 'They must be cross because we left without saying goodbye.'

There were still air raids. The German planes bombed the town on their way to the Russian front, and discharged surplus bombs on their way back. The American planes chased them. Esther felt she could not fight any more. Whatever would happen would happen, and there was nothing she could do about it.

Esther and Myra slept in a bed left by the Germans, and when a bombardment would start they would crouch under the solitary table in the empty room. It was warm even at night by then and there was no need for a thick duvet. The primus was still in the kitchen.

Esther went out every day in search of petrol for the lamp and light a fire, some maize flour, some sour milk and some eggs. On the way back she stopped at Grandma Anna's house. The kind woman understood and had long forgiven her leaving without a word. The two women embraced each other crying. At the police station, Esther filled in the necessary forms and paid the fine with money Grandpa gave her. After about a week of fear and cold, noise and loneliness the papers arrived. This time they left for good, by train. Clara came to the station to say goodbye. 'It will soon be over,' she said. 'The Russians are near the border.'

10
THE END OF THE WAR

Myra and Esther were back in the lovely house on the lovely street. Myra could not wait for the morrow to see her darling Lux again.

The next day she woke up, said her prayer with Grandma Risll and went to the garden. Myra waited quietly, busying herself near Grandpa until Esther finished cutting fresh flowers. Mama looked happy and relaxed.

As soon as Esther left, Myra placed herself at her observation post. She waited and waited and saw all the soldiers, but neither Lux nor his handler appeared or marched with the others.

All morning she wondered were Lux was and why she didn't see him, but she could not ask anyone.. In the middle of the meal Grandpa suddenly said to Esther, 'Do you remember that German shepherd dog they had? It was shot. The other day I was watering the garden when a German grandee arrived in a car. The Jerries lined themselves up on the steps, and this important commander, the big Hun, got out. The dog and the soldier in charge were first in the line, saluting. The dog started barking and showing his big teeth, so the Ober-what'sit took out a revolver and shot the dog dead. They all went inside, leaving the dead dog sprawled out in the street. The animals!'

Myra could not contain herself. She burst into tears and ran to her room.

The war was coming to an end. New planes were passing overhead. There was talk that they were Americans going to bomb Ploesti and other important places. On the way there and on the way back a few bombs strayed and hit Focsani as well.

Early one morning Myra was woken by someone shouting outside: 'Esther! Esther! It's me!'

Esther got up. 'You stay where you are,' she ordered Myra. In the next room she could hear Grandma was up and moving about.

Myra raised her head, trying to hear the voices. Doors were banging, hurried steps to and fro, a clatter of dishes. Myra could bear not knowing what was happening. Curiosity got the better of her. She quietly crept out of bed and tip-toed to the kitchen window. Her eyes grew big with wonder. There they were, Mama and Grandma, throwing buckets of water over a man who stood outside. From time to time Grandma poured vinegar and petrol from bottles into the water.

The man was younger than Grandpa, much younger. His round head was shaved. He was wearing a dirty grey vest and long johns. He stood uncomplaining as the water hit his head and poured all over him. Myra could not stifle a scream when, as she crept out closer and closer, she saw small grey insects running out from every fold of the man's garments.

Mama turned. Her eyes were full of tears which started running down her face.

'Don't come out, go back to bed,' she shouted.Myra ran inside.

Grandpa stood by the door. ' Come in, child! This is your father, Usher. There's nothing to worry about. He's just full of lice and we can't let him in the house until we clean him,' he said. The million little grey insects crawled hurriedly down in Indian file. Myra went back to bed but climbed up on the window ledge where she could catch a view of what was happening outside.

Myra looked at the man again. Could this beggar be her father? So skinny and small! She remembered him a big strong man with curly hair!

Grandpa came into her room.

'Grandpa, is it true? Is this my father?'

'Yes darling. He just came back. Isn't it a miracle? We should rejoice.'

'But Grandpa, why doesn't he have any proper clothes on?'

'Because he comes from far away, all the way from a concentration camp. He must have left at night in the clothes he was in. Be patient. When he is clean and rested he will tell us all about it, I'm sure.'

'What are lice? Were the lice in the camp too?'

'Yes, wherever there are many people and dirt, lice come too, and bring dreadful diseases.'

'Is that man ill?'

'Let's hope not. That's why Mum and Grandma are trying to clean him.up All in good time! Be patient!'

61

A bright sun rose and in the distance. In the street, the German soldiers started their daily routine, marching up and down.

The women let Usher come into the entrance hall. Voices were lowered to a whisper: no need to draw attention.

Usher came in smelling of pungent petrol mixed with vinegar. Myra was reluctant to go near him.This was not the Daddy she once knew. Esther put food on the table and the man started eating, so fast that Myra wondered how anybody could be that hungry. More food was put in front of him and he gulped that down too.

'Perhaps that's enough for now,' said Esther. 'It will make you ill, if you haven't eaten for days.'

Usher was dressed in Grandpa's pyjamas, which hung loosely on him, and went to bed. He slept for a day and a night, and then over breakfast he told his story.

He was taken to a camp in the Ukraine, beyond the River Bug, somewhere near Treblinka. In time he became friendly with a Ukrainian guard who had warned him of what was going to happen to the camp. The camp doctor, a Jewish man from Galatzi, was told the same story.

As the Russian army came nearer each day, the camp commandant decided to kill all the inmates and burn down the camp so that no trace of it could be found. The younger and fitter prisoners decided they would try to escape. So it happened that the night their Ukrainian friend was on duty, they handed him their meagre possessions and gained their freedom. They ran into the forest, with only the ragged night clothes they were wearing.

The escapees did not know their way home, so they decided to follow the railway track that ran all the way from Kishinew south into Romania. Usher slept in the open and for a few nights he was given shelter in a stable by some peasants. Sometimes he was asked to help with the harvest, which he did in exchange for food and shelter. None of the farmers denounced the escapees to the police or to the army, although they knew they were Jewish and had come from the camp.

Slowly Usher found his way home, safe and sound, but it took a long time for him to get close to his daughter. Every time he tried to embrace her she ran away, or hid behind her mother. Esther did not encourage Myra to go near her father. Tight-lipped, Esther walked around the house, did her chores and said nothing. Nor did she make any gesture towards Usher. He was trying to kiss and cuddle both mother and daughter, but an invisible barrier separated them.

'Give them time,' Grandpa said in Yiddish to his wife.

A week or two passed and Myra sensed an unease settling on the household. Grandpa made some comments, implying that Usher should start getting some work. Money and food were dwindling fast, with so many mouths to feed.

Esther and Usher started arguing, first in whispers, and then louder and louder.

'Did you fool around while I was away?' Usher asked.

'How dare you!' Ester was angry.

'Why, then, are you so cold towards me?'

'Just take it easy, there. It has had been such a long time, we all went through such a lot. And you know I don't want any more children.'

'Where did you get the lipstick? Who are you making yourself attractive for?' His old jealousy surfaced again.

'Oi, shut up! You even frighten the child. You are going about like a bull in a china shop.'

'I see you and your mother and father have put ideas into her head, so she does not come near me.'

'What an ungrateful thing to say, after they looked after us so well.'

'Yes, and they put all this religious crap into her head.'

'Stop swearing! Just because you are an illiterate fool, without any religious feeling, it doesn't mean she has to grow up the same.'

Myra grew increasingly quiet. She believed it was all her fault that her Muma and Daddy were unhappy. She quietly withdrew into herself and spent most of the day watching the soldiers across the road.

What interested her was that every day for a week they brought in other soldiers under guard, the German soldiers pointing their guns at the new ones. The new ones wore brown uniforms, not very smart, and they walked with their heads down. From time to time they were hurried along and prodded in their back with a German bayonet. They did not have weapons.

'Who are they?' Myra asked

'They are Russian prisoners. See, they have no guns or belts,' said Usher.

'Were you pushed like that, Daddy?'

'Yes. And worse.'

'Why are the Germans always so cruel?'

'Because there is a war on and Hitler, their leader, orders them to be cruel, especially towards Jews.'

Myra was thinking of the soldier who gave her chocolate, and wondered if all Germans were the same.

Extract from Usher's Memorandum to the Conference of Compensation:

In 1939, I was called to rejoin my Regiment, Regiment one fusiliers, in Iasi, Romania. In 1940/41 during an attempted *putsch* of the right wing of the Iron Guard, I was hounded by a gang of legionnaires, beaten up, robbed of my uniform and rifle and, battered and bruised, I sought refuge in an alcohol factory in Iasi, across the road from the railway station. I was cared for by some workers at the factory, including the factory engineer who was an ethnic German. I rejoined my regiment. After that I had changed my name to Victor Ursou and had a spell of relative tranquillity. However after June 1941, all Jews were expelled from the armed forces, this time every one, and I returned home to my wife and child in Barlad, only to find that my home was taken over as lodgings for Romanian Officers. In 1942 I was rounded up and sent to a forced labour camp. Initially at Lacul-Sarat-Braila, then Vaslui and then moved to Bolgrad and Tighina, Taraclea and Chisinau, all in Bassarabia . We worked on buildings, maintained roads and railways and lived either in huts or in summer out in the open next to the sites we were working on.

I had in 1942 already foregone most of my assets in an attempt to avoid forced labour, but to no avail. In June 1944,when the German defence lines in Eastern Russia and the Ukraine were broken, there were strong rumours that all Jews would be rounded up and sent to the camps which were then known as the death camps. In August '44, our camp was overrun by the Russians and we were set free. I made my way back from Tighina in Basarabia to Barlad on foot, eating scraps and what I could steal from the fields or work for farmers.

Usher went out every day, once he had recovered, to look for work, but he could not find any because he did not have the right papers.

Then one very hot morning, Myra as usual went to her observation post. Her eyes grew large in wonder. A great change seemed to have taken place. The German soldiers, only yesterday so proud in their green uniforms, today were dishevelled, without their guns or belts, and were sweeping the streets. It was late summer and the leaves had started to fall and cover the ground. Guarding them were the large men with their thick moustaches, smoking their pipes and looking on. Only yesterday they had been the prisoners, and now they had changed places.

Myra ran indoors to tell Mum. Just then Usher came in, all smiles.

'We are free,' he shouted, waving the newspaper he had bought.

'Armistice Day! The King has signed!'

He lifted Mama and whirled her round the room, then Myra, then he kissed Grandma. Everyone was shedding tears of happiness. It was the 23 of August 1944, the end of the war for Romania. Today they were safe. Tomorrow - we had to wait and see what that might bring.

11
AFTER THE WAR

Times were uncertain. Usher found a way to earn money by buying and selling goods. Each morning he went to the railway station and met Russian soldiers who were selling pieces of jewellery looted from houses they had ransacked on their way to Berlin. Usher started by exchanging his wristwatch for pieces of jewellery. He sold the jewellery for more watches The Russians were very keen to have watches – some of them had never owned one.and they would pay with the looted pieces.

Usher would bring the pieces of jewellery to show the family, who looked with wonder at rings in gold and white gold with precious stones, heavy gold chains and brooches encrusted with diamonds and rubies. First he would offer them to Esther and make her wear them for a few days. Then he would sell them for flour and bread and corn and beans and more watches.

Esther was only too happy to renounce the rich gems which adorned her fingers and neck. She preferred to have food on the table and she was pleased when Usher brought enough for the whole family. Hunger was the main enemy now, and one could not eat gold or precious stones, no matter how beautiful they were.

Another day, Usher brought home a white silk parachute which was so large he had to drag it home. Esther and her parents gathered round looking and touching the shiny, sturdy, creamy white fabric. They had never seen anything like it. 'What happened to the person who brought this down? Was he Russian, German or American?'

'I have no idea. What does it matter? He is probably dead by now. Do you like it'?

Esther opened the divan bed and from the very bottom took out her store of pattern books. With the silk she made a skirt for herself and blouses for Grandma, and Myra had a skirt made from the remnants.

Not long after, Usher had news that people had discovered large stores of food in caves abandoned by the Germans when they left the town in a hurry. Together with most of the other inhabitants, he broke into the caves and took as much of the food as each one could carry before the Russians who were in town found out.

The Russian advance troops were just as hungry as the civilians. One day they killed the few swans that had swum in the town park for many years past. They built a fire in the middle of the town market place and put a large pot on it to cook. The cooking went on and on and the swan's meat was tough. People gathered around and watched. It is said that it took three days to tenderise the meat. In the end the soldiers ate it tough as it was.

Usher came home from the caves laden with meat in tins, vegetables, chocolate powder, milk, even oranges. Myra had never tasted oranges before, and did not think much of the pungent

69

fruit. Esther was worried that grandpa, a devout Jew, would object that not kosher food was brought into his house. But neither of Esther's parents seemed to notice or raise any objections. It was horse meat, and it tasted good and they were hungry. A few days later, in passing, Risl said that she knew from her mother's teachings that what goes into the mouth was not a sin, what comes out of the mouth is a sin. Myra wondered what that meant.

One day the front rooms were opened. Grandpa Moishe had received a letter from the owner of the villa saying the family was never coming back. The owner wanted to sell the house and all the goods stored in the front rooms were a gift to them for the good care they took of the property.

It was like an Aladdin's Cave. To Myra it looked like an enchanted palace; the walls were covered with roses and leaves painted on silk; some walls were entirely covered in wood panels and in the panels portraits of people in oval frames; beautiful ladies and handsome men in uniform looked at Myra. There were chairs and seats stacked up covered with large pieces of fabric, a large chest full of linen and silk and glass and on top a large doll with golden hair and frilly skirts and petticoats. Esther took some beautiful vases, embroidered table cloth, silver cutlery and glasses finely engraved with flowers. Myra was given the beautiful big doll with golden hair. Her eyes opened and closed and she squeaked 'Mama' when her tummy was pressed. To go with the doll there was a doll's pram with an embroidered cushion and a duvet. Myra held the doll and looked at it with wonder. She had never had a doll except for the rag doll her mother made her. She was not used to playing with dolls and soon dismantled her to see where the squeak came from. After that she lost interest and returned to her little book and her slate.

Children grown old before their time, during years of war, brought up without ordinary comforts, unused to playing with toys, not savouring the taste of oranges; adults who would gladly exchange gold and diamonds for a meal and a roof over their head: those were the values of that time.

There was freedom to move around without fear of falling bombs, without fear of being abused or even killed for being a Jew or a Gypsy. Those worries were replaced by the fear of looting or women being abused by the invading Russians. No man or woman could wear a watch in public without having it snatched by a Russian soldier. It became a national joke; Russian soldiers wearing four or five watches at once and stopping to work out what time it was.

The family moved back home, to the house Moishe built in Pescaria Veche, near the market. Esther, Usher and Myra, not having anywhere else to live, moved in with them. The house was much smaller. The front room, where Grandpa had his workshop, was converted into a bedroom for Esther and Usher. The middle room was

Grandma's and Grandpa's. The little room was for Myra . The kitchen was the place they all shared.

A Russian commander came soon after they had moved back in and asked if a few soldiers could spend the night there. Grandpa said yes. This was the least they could do for the liberators who saved their lives. Beds were made up in the kitchen for the three young men. As soon as Grandma fed them all, one pulled his balalaika out of his sack and started playing, while the others joined in the singing. The family stood around looking in wonder at these very young boys, so far away from home, singing songs of their beloved country.

One of them pointed to the mezuzah stuck on the door. Then he opened his tunic and   round his neck was a chain on which a Zion-pendant hung next to his rank and number. The next morning the soldiers left.

Almost daily a Russian sergeant accom-panied by a few soldiers came to inspect every house in the street. As a precaution, Grandpa kept an eye on their approach and warned the women to hide at the back of the house, just in case. Rumours were circulating that the soldiers rape women. The soldiers came in, advanced from room to room so Grandma and Esther bent their heads low so as not to be seen through the windows and stayed outside the house .The soldiers inspected the first rooms and as they advanced, the women holding Myra tight by the hand advanced as well towards the back door . Then they stopped outside in the narrow yard and walked under the windows towards the front and came in through the front door while the patrol exited through the back.. This moving in a circle, like a dance, went round two, three times. When occasionally the Russians turned unexpectedly straight into the kitchen everybody froze. Myra remembers one such time.

Grandma was cooking. A big pot of soup was bubbling on the stove for the Sabbath. It was a Friday. Esther was peeling potatoes and Grandpa was saying his morning prayers wearing his shawl, called a tallit, white with black stripes and silk fringes, a leather strap twisted round to hold one of his tefilla on his arm. The second tefilla rested on his forehead. When the Russian officer entered the kitchen, everyone remained fixed like statues.

The officer reached above the stove, took down a big ladle from its hook, and dipped it into the boiling soup. He said something in Russian. They assumed it was, 'Let's see what's cooking.' The only words they understood were 'harasho' and 'davay'. And he drank, not even flinching from the heat.

'Harasho, ocheni harasho,' he said, smacking his lips. He invited the three soldiers to taste. They helped themselves copiously, then they all saluted and left.

'Is there anything left, Grandma?' Myra asked.

'Not much. Just potatoes. We'll fry some onions and it will be all right.'

Esther started laughing out loud.

'Good job he didn't touch you, mother. He would have found you covered in gold chains and watches.'

'You can talk,' she said. 'Thank God they were not doing what everybody in town says they are doing, the animals. Have you seen how they eat? Like pigs!'

Soon after, at the beginning of winter 1946, the Russians began to settle in. They brought their wives and children. It was quite a spectacle, and the townspeople watched in amazement. The women wore coats in the fashion of the Great War, little high heeled boots and fur hats and collars. These people, Esther explained, remained in the fashion of 1917, when the Russian Revolution occurred; since then the borders had been closed to the outside world. No newspapers or films from outside Russia were allowed. So the women were dressed as Anna Karenina might have been.

There were new neighbours in Pescaria Veche, a young Russian couple with a small child. They smiled when passing by and said something that nobody understood. Each afternoon, when the house chores were finished, Grandma and Myra would install themselves in the front window and observe the street. They laughed each time the Russian couple returned home from their meeting place, quite drunk, quarrelling, the little baby screaming, sometimes being held upside down. Grandma would exchange laughs with the neighbour across the road, who was spending her

74

time watching the same. Studying the Russians behind closed doors became their favourite passtime.

Years of war away from home brought a shortage of men. So many had died in the war, there was a shortage of tools, their horses and oxen perished – all these things, together with the inclement weather, deepened the years of famine. The town was starving. The occupying Russians opened their bread stores and distributed dark sour bread to the people. Myra went each morning to queue at the bread shop. Ration coupons were distributed and Usher started trading in these, besides his commerce with the soldiers.

In spite of his efforts to keep them fed, Usher did not endear himself to Esther's family. He continued to be the uneducated outsider, the 'goy', because he did not practice the rituals of the Jewish faith and he was the one to light the fire on Sabbath.

'Daddy, why are you not going to Shull?' Myra asked.

'What shall I do there, among all those people who stayed at home while I nearly lost my life in the camps?'

'But Grandfather says you should stay at home on Friday evenings and Saturdays.'

'And who is going to queue for bread and go to the Saturday market? I'm fed up with his rituals, he who gave up his work so early, expecting everyone to keep him while he does his praying.'

'But how come you can't speak Yiddish?'

'Because I speak Romanian. I am from Moldavia and I speak with the words I was raised. My mother and father spoke Romanian and so do I.'

'Stop teaching the child bad things,' Esther admonished him. But Usher carried on: 'I didn't like school much. When my father appointed an old rabbi to teach me and my brothers the sidur. my brother Millu learned everything by heart, and so did Gus. But I kept playing with the old man's beard. Boy, what a beating my father gave me! Then I ran away'

'Usher, I told you to stop!' Esther was getting angry.'

'How old were you?'

'About 14. Just after my bar-mitzvah.' What a story that was. Milou came behind me to whisper the words.' Usher smiled at the distant memory.

Esther's loyalties were increasingly divided. She lived with her parents and had to respect their ways, but she agreed with Usher. She said it was time that Jewish people assimilated and became properly part of Romania, so that pogroms and concentration camps wouldn't happen again. The grandparents were taken aback when Esther and Usher declared their intent of placing Myra in the local school; Grandfather was insistent that she should join the recently opened Jewish primary school. But Esther stood firm: her children would be integrated. The rift between Myra's parents and her grandparents deepened. Living so close together did not help. Usher resented the grandparents. He thought they treated Esther like a servant. Grandma left all the heavy housework to Esther while she spent increasing amounts of time across the road with her friends and neighbours, speaking ill of Usher.

Myra felt the tension and uneasiness and retreated into herself again, finding comfort in her ABC books. She also learned to knit from Grandma and spent long hours making a never-ending scarf. She became friendly and started visiting the neighbours. She went to see Viorica and her sister across the road. They were the teenage daughters of the wine merchant. The two girls played with her as if she was a doll, making her lips red with lipstick and frizzing her hair. It was lovely to be pampered. The old lady next door was also kind to Myra and told her stories about her son, who was a well-known doctor in Bucharest, and about all the faraway places she used to travel before the war.

Summer passed. The hot winds blew away the withered flower heads, spreading their seeds far and wide. The earth cracked in uneven diamond patterns, leaving gaps as deep as a pit. The pavements melted and gave way under the weight of the women's high-heeled shoes. Then came the floods, which ended the monotony of heat and dust.

Usher found work in a timber yard. The pay was low but he didn't mind, as he knew he would manage; he would find a little business on the side. The famine bit hard. People were selling heirlooms, books clothes, jewellery for a few kilograms of maize flour. The sour taste from the Russian bakery brought people out queuing for hours. Although they kept grumbling that the bread was heavy and sour, they ate it all the same, dreaming of the white fluffy bread they used to have.

In 1947 the first election after the war took place. Posters were put on every lamppost. Many were displayed on people's windows. Some were depicting a large yellow sun with a happy smile, others, a large eye looking straight through one's face.

This of course, made Myra curious, she wanted to know what was all this talk in the house or whenever Esther met with the neighbours. Usher explained patiently: 'The sun is the face of the new party, the social democrats. The eye represents the old guard, the conservative and the national farmers party.'

It did not make much sense to Myra. 'Which party are you going to vote for, Daddy?

'For the sun of course. Who else can a Jew, just out of a concentration camp vote for? For the old guard allied with the fascists who wanted to exterminate us?'

Little did he know or expect that the victorious social democrats together with the communists controlled by the Soviets would oust the King soon after the elections and replace him with the republican regime of terror that followed. Indeed, they could not imagine that behind the smiley face of the sun, there were heavy clouds of storm hiding.

Then, out of nowhere, a new law was passed: money was devalued, with no prior warning. The aim was to stabilise the currency and ensure equality for all. It affected rich and poor alike: the old who had saved for their pension; the soldiers returning from the war, whose wives dutifully saved their service pay for when they came back; the landowners and the black market racketeers.

Every adult had the right to exchange no more than 1,000 units of the old money called lei for 100 new lei. Whatever surplus anyone possessed was worthless, only good for lighting the fire or cleaning windows. But it didn't affect Esther or the grandparents. They didn't have any money.

Instead, for a fee, enterprising Usher found other people who asked him to change their surplus money. So he exchanged 1,000 in his name, another 1,000 on behalf of Esther, another of behalf of Grandpa, and also of Grandma. Each transaction made him a little profit. Usher felt pleased with himself, while others felt a little different.

At the end of 1945, Esther gave birth to a baby and Myra had not even noticed that her mother was pregnant. Myra was busy with her new life and Esther never mentioned that there would be a new baby or prepared her for such an event. She was secretive and made every effort not to show her growing tummy. The baby girl was born one night in the front room of Pescaria Veche. Esther gave birth assisted by her mother, without much fuss.

Myra was woken up by the commotion, doors opened and closed, people walking to and fro. She waited to see what was happening. Usher came in the room and told her that a baby girl was born and Myra had a sister. She could not wait to meet the new arrival.

'This is your sister,' Grandma said and introduced the new baby. She was so little, with a clean white complexion and rosy cheeks, a small mouth and long eyelashes, She was asleep nestled at Mama's breast.

'She is so pretty, Mama. I'll call her Dolly.'

Esther smiled and said, 'See what a present I had made for you?'

Usher joined them, and embraced all of them. 'This baby is a good omen, you will see, all will be well from now on.'

'Was I a good omen too, when I was born, Daddy?' Usher did not answer.

Myra's eyes filled with tears. Esther noticed and reached out to her. 'It was not your fault, darling, it just happened that way, you were born before the war, and she is born now, when there is peace. We love both.' But the bitter taste stayed with Myra for many years to come.

The baby was named Brucha as she was born on the second day of the Jewish New Year, but she remained Dolly for Myra, for the family and all the close friends although officially she was Bea. When she grew up she insisted that she should be called Bea. Dolly was pretty, and more so with each day that passed. She was adored by all. Esther devoted all her time to Dolly, from bath time to breastfeeding, to play and cuddles. Myra watched in wonder. Esther no longer told her stories or taught her to read, she was too busy singing to the baby. Dolly made quick progress. She soon sat up, talked early and started walking before her first birthday. Myra loved her too, but she also felt a little jealous, displaced from her mother and father's attention.

In September of 1946 Myra eagerly waited to go to school and her wish was granted. She was accepted for the local school, the same school that her mother had gone to. She was younger than the others but she was accepted.

The mornings got chilly and Myra did not have a coat but she had an all-in-one suit that Uncle Leon sent as a present .The shoes did not fit her growing feet so she went on her wellies.They had holes in the soles and they made a sound swoosh, swoosh, when Myra stepped into a paddle. But Mrs Christmas, the teacher, was nice to her. Myra was eager to learn and she could already read. Mama made her a nice uniform, a little black pinafore dress, with a white embroidered collar ending with a big red ribbon in a bow under her chin. She was so proud! Mrs Christmas sat her in the front row, she was smaller than most of her class. Myra was not used to children, she had not attended any nursery school and she was a little timid at first. The other girls knew things she did not know; they all knew the prayer Our Father, they signed themselves with the cross and one girl sang beautifully the national anthem. 'Long live the King, in peace and in honour,' she sang. Each morning Esther took Myra to school, carrying in a bag two pieces of wood for the fire. Each child had to bring wood to the class. The teacher would lit the fire in the large terra-cotta stove, the classroom filled up with smoke and everyone started coughing. It took a long time for the stove to warm up. By the time the air cleared and the classroom was warm, it was time to go home. Once a week there was a lesson in Religion Education. The teacher was the local priest, Father Ivan. He was a big man with a booming voice. During the first, or perhaps the second week, he asked Myra to stand up.

'You are Jewish, aren't you? What is your name?' He smiled a friendly smile.

Myra told him yes, suddenly feeling guilty for no particular reason. The whole class was looking at her.

'I thought so,' he said. 'With those large eyes and dark curly hair,you remind me of a young calf. You had better go outside and wait till we finish our lesson.' Myra stood up and left with her head down, followed by the eyes of the whole class. She stayed outside the door and felt lonely and rejected. Every week she stood there, listening and repeating all that was said inside the class. By the end of the first year she knew all the prayers by heart.

12
THE BIG CHANGE

Myra and Dolly were given new clothes and new shoes as Usher started to earn better. They were so happy. Their understanding of the world was within the limits of what happened within their family.

Esther took her two girls to the photographer to have their pictures taken in their new clothes. She was so proud. She sent copies to her brothers and to Grandma Anna.

School started again the following September, and many changes confronted the young pupils. The school was no longer called the Rahtivan Preparatory, after the name of the previous headmistress. It became Elementary School Number 4. Romania's flag no longer flew above the roof of the building. Instead there was a red flag with a hammer and sickle planted in the main entrance next to the plain red, yellow and blue flag of the new Popular Republic of Romania. The Elena-Queen Mother High School was now named the Lyceum Alexander Ion Cuza for girls. All those changes took place because in the year 1947 King Michael of Romania abdicated and left the country.

There were no more prayers in assembly. Ada, with her large chain and silver cross on her chest, no longer stood up proudly reciting 'Our Father…' Instead there were slogans: 'Long Live the Party and its People,' 'Long Live the Soviet Union, the Bastion of Peace.' The children had to learn the words of the 'International,' and a new national anthem.

The next task of the New Order was to remove all signs of the old. The first week back at school, the teacher told everyone to bring to school a pair of scissors. With the scissors every pupil was asked to cut out from their books every image of the King, the Queen and any other dignitaries, every picture of the Royal Palaces, churches and monasteries, any prints of the National Emblem with the King's head and all songs or verses which contained words of the old regime.

Page by page, the books acquired hollow windows staring back at the children, blind openings into a future no child could glimpse. Page by page, Myra cut the paper windows, erasing the past. With Elena, her desk mate, and Sonya, who sat in front of her, she started a game. Each of the girls had to remember who or what was in the frame before the picture was cut out. They wanted to preserve the memory of their time, never out loud, only in whispers.

When their task was completed the teacher asked the children to call their parents 'Comrade Mother' and 'Comrade Father'.

Families were no longer supposed to go to church on Sundays or Holy Days. Christmas became 'Winter Break' and Father Christmas became 'Grandfather Frost'.

School life continued normally, adjusting itself to the changes. The teacher remained her old self, welcoming all the children into her class and getting on with teaching them the 3Rs. She dutifully taught the children that the important people were no longer called Mister or Miss or Mistress, they were to be spoken of as Comrade. Nothing more was heard from Father Ivan, and there were no more religious education lessons. Later on, Esther found out from one of her friends, that father Ivan had been arrested and deported to Siberia for being a Nazi sympathiser.' 'Fancy that, she said, I knew him for a long time,Such a nice man'

The new leaders were: Comrade Dej, Comrade Anna Powker and Comrade Kishinewsky, who had recently returned from the Soviet Union. They had taken refuge there during the war as hounded communists and once there, they helped to form a new battalion of soldiers from the prisoners of war and 'turned their arms against the Germans and fought to see Romania free.'

'They returned heroes and leaders to teach the new ways. In the light of the teachings of Marx and Engels, Lenin and Stalin,' Comrade-Mrs Christmas taught the class and the girls had to repeat those words after her. Myra reported to her mother, 'From now on we shall no longer celebrate the Holy Trinity, but the Pillars of the New Democratic Society: Marx, Engels, Lenin and Stalin.'

'I'm glad to hear it,' said Esther. 'You haven't missed anything, then, by not learning about Jesus and Mary and the Holy Spirit.' Usher just shook his head and frowned.

When Myra came home from school calling her 'Comrade Mother,' Esther could not stifle a laugh, and when Dolly did the same, copying Myra, both parents roared with laughter. When he recovered, Usher took Myra aside and very seriously told her never to talk at school or to anyone about that little moment of mirth.

Everyday life did not became easier with all those changes. Of course, there were winners and losers. The very poor peasants acquired a small piece of land. The low-paid workers, whether or not they had knowledge or experience, were put in positions of leadership and supervision, particularly if they joined the Party.

Usher found a steady job. As he had experience, he was put in charge of the timber yard, which was taken from its owners and nationalised. He stopped short of becoming a Communist Party member because he did not trust them. He thought they were cruel. As a result another man, a Mr Wise was put on general duties.

Other people, the ones who lost money and property, those who were once rich and well-to-do, were arrested, or they could be seen on the street corners, trying to sell domestic objects or their once-fashionable clothes in order to feed their families. Many landowners, industry leaders, writers, clergy were detained as capitalists exploiters or fascist sympathisers. Prisoners were sent to work on the new Danube-Black Sea canal or the salt mines. Many never returned.

13
MOVING HOME

Home life became increasingly difficult because of the conflict between the younger members of the family with their new ways and the older parents stuck in their traditional way of life, That reached the height of tension when one Friday evening, at the end of a hard week, Usher brought home their first radio set. Eager to install and hear it working, he set to work and soon music and talk filled the room. At that point the door from the grandparents' room opened and Risll came out, screaming, 'Blasphemy!' It was a Friday night, the beginning of the Sabbath, how dare they? The next day Usher found a house to rent and with Esther and their two children moved out.

Now Esther had her own home and she was very house proud. Everything in that house had to be clean and tidy to perfection. Not a thing could be moved or disturbed without her permission. In the morning, be it winter or summer, the pillows, the night dresses, the pyjamas, the bed covers had to go outside on the line to be aired. Each piece of furniture was swept clean and polished daily. The chairs were put upside down on the table, the carpets were removed, taken out into the yard, beaten and shaken. Esther then crawled on all fours and polished the floors. Then, the pieces were put back in the reverse order; carpets and chairs returned to position, beds made, and surfaces dusted again in the perpetual rhythmic ritual.

If the children   disturbed her order, she would start screaming and threatening and the children would cover their ears and cower in a corner, remaining silent till the crisis had abated.

Esther was not keen to have the girls' friends around, and if they did come occasionally they would play outside rather than come in the house, for fear of making a mess. What was she trying to prove? Many years after, Myra thought of those times and wondered if her mother was deeply depressed and blamed herself for not being more understanding.

Outside the home, terror reigned. Everybody was suspicious of everybody else. There was not a single person who knew whether or not he or she would be 'lifted' during the night by the secret police. Esther prepared a suitcase with all essentials for Usher, just in case, just as she had done in 1942. This time they were prepared.

Parents no longer dared to be open with their children. A wall of silence arose between members of families out of fear. Young people were encouraged at school or at the new Pioneers Club to tell about home life. A newborn child was christened in secret, one of the few remaining priests being invited to come to the house and carry out the ceremony hidden in the cellar or the loft, away from prying neighbours or talkative children. Many Jewish boys were no longer circumcised, and bar mitzvahs took place in the family home, behind closed doors, if at all.

Myra was adamant that the family should no longer visit Grandma and Grandpa. 'I'm not going,' she said, stamping her foot. 'Grandpa is doing those silly prayers every day, and keeping the old Jewish festivals. These are the old bourgeois practices that fed capitalism,' she chanted.

Dolly joined in and said, 'They are bad. I saw Grandma has white bread cholas hidden in the cupboard, but when we got visiting she gives us cold polenta and marmalade. Yuk!'

'Shut up, you two,' said Esther.'She must have had a parcel from Uncle Leon.'

Esther spoke to Usher when the girls went out to play. 'What are we going to do with them?'

'Keep quiet. Don't tell them off. Myra may go back to school and tell all. Leave them alone. They'll grow out of it. As for your mother, I don't doubt what Dolly is saying is true.'

In 1949 the grandparents invited the family for a meal. As tradition demanded, the candles were lit and after prayers, bits of chola dipped in salt were shared out by Grandpa. Grandma prepared a tasty chicken soup with *kneidlech*, dumplings made of egg and flour. Then she served the chicken pieces with cooked haricot beans as a side dish. She also put on the table a dish of sour cherries cooked with sugar. The children were given *sacherlech* cookies which she had baked for Shabbat. When the Shabbat meal was finished, the grandparents told Esther they intended to emigrate to Israel. Leon, their younger son, had arranged it all. First they would join their other son, Abraham, who had lived in Israel since the beginning of the war. Then the eldest brother, Jean and his wife Peppy and their son Karol would go, and if all was well, the second son Isaac and his wife Golda would follow.

The plan was for Leon to put his affairs in order and be the last to leave.

Esther stood very still and quiet for a while. She had to let the news sink in.

When she had recovered from the first shock she said: 'This is a surprise. Why wasn't I asked?'

'Well,' they said, 'Leon arranged it all, and he knew you wouldn't want to leave Romania. You said so before.'

Usher put his arm round his wife's shoulder.

'It's *bon voyage*, then,' he said to the grandparents and made as if to leave.

'Before you go,' said Grandpa in an embarrassed voice, 'This house belongs to Leon now. He said you could move back if you want to, free of charge.'

That's big of him, Usher thought. Now that I've lost all the money I got from selling what remained of our house!

The family returned to Pescaria Veche, to the small house where the rooms run into one another, all painted white with a dark blue lower border, with the narrow garden of cobbled stones, that ran the length of the house, and the little flower border with primroses and sweet peas and petunias.

Esther felt deeply hurt. She felt humiliated and although she had had her quarrels with her mother since they lived together during the last months of the war, she felt almost bereaved. Already she missed them. She felt lonely and rejected. She had no friends. Her school friends had gone their different ways and she never approached them because she felt embarrassed to have Usher, such a coarse, unsociable man, by her side.

There were no other relatives in the town, except an old distant cousin and her husband. When she was a girl at home she had been friendly with the couple's daughters, but they married in different parts of the country and the thread was broken. A deep crease appeared on Esther's forehead as she frowned more. Her blue eyes were more grey, her lips thinner and thinner. She put on weight as the family became more prosperous. Increasingly she relied on her daughters for friendship and company.

Esther never spoke to her parents again. She never answered letters written by Abraham, her brother who lived in Palestine since the beginning of the Second World War and she never shed a tear when she had learned that her father had died in Israel of cancer.

Usher, although he had never got on with Esther's parents, tried to persuade her to keep in touch with her family, but she cut them off completely and for ever. She kept in touch with her other brothers while they were still in Romania until they too, left.

Once a year Esther took the girls to Bucharest to visit their uncles. They went to stay with Uncle

Isack and Aunt Golda. They lived in an elegant apartment in the middle of Bucharest, near the park. They did not have children of their own and the girls had to be on their best behaviour.

Occasionally, the family was invited to Uncle Leon's house and the girls liked that best. Uncle Leon sent his black car to fetch them, and they were driven to the elegant mansion by the chauffeur. Uncle Leon lived there with his beautiful wife Sophie and their two daughters. The children had a German governess to look after them, as Uncle Leon was busy with his factory and Aunt Sophie was busy with the dressmaker, shopping, and having piano lessons. Myra and Dolly liked being there a lot because they could play and do whatever they liked and Tetta, as the governess was called, took them to the parks and on walks.

As planned, Leon was the last to leave. He had matters to settle. The first was to divorce his wife. On their last visit to the capital city, Myra and Dolly could hardly wait to meet their cousins Vivy and Gaby, but there was a surprise for them. Leon's wife, Aunt Sophie, had left or, more likely, she had been made to leave, and Vivy and Gaby were being cared for by Tetta. The girls were miserable and missed their mother.

On the journey home Esther explained to Myra and Dolly that Uncle Leon was going to marry again and the girls would have a new mother.

'The miserable sod,' she could not prevent herself from exclaiming between gritted teeth.

It seems that Leon had had a relationship with his new wife-to-be for some years. He had even bought her an apartment.

'What's a relationship?' piped Dolly.

'You keep quiet,' snapped Myra.

Esther told the girls that the new wife was Leon's childhood sweetheart. She was older than he was. When he was 18, he wanted to marry her, but Grandpa had forbidden him. She was a year or two older than he was, and she was not from a good family, by his standards.

Leon cried and begged his father to change his mind, but the old man never did and he obeyed.

He never stopped loving that woman and although a few years later he married pretty Aunt Sophie, his heart belonged to his first sweetheart.

Events turned bad for Uncle Leon and the children. His factory was nationalised and he was charged with gross embezzlement. He and Annie and the children tried to leave the country but the private ship they hired was intercepted and Leon was arrested.

Sophie wrote to Esther giving her the sad news that the children were back living with her, because Leon's new wife did not feel they were her responsibility. Sophie was happy to have her daughters back, but she needed help.

Usher, who was a generous man, was first to offer assistance. He sent Sophie some money and later food parcels. Sophie found work in a bakery and Gaby and Vivy started school.

14
PROSPERITY

Esther and Usher started to prosper under the new regime. People needed homes. After the war the country people had to repair or rebuild farms and homes damaged or destroyed in the fighting, but the supply of building materials was never enough to satisfy demand.

A back-hander economy developed and Usher started to save materials for the people who paid him in cash. He brought the cash home to Esther who kept the accounts for him and looked after the money.

This money was to enable his family to live better. His salary was pitifully small, but with the extra cash he could buy meat from the butcher who, for a sum, would put aside a good cut in his cold room for Usher or for anybody else who could afford to pay. It was the same with the baker, who might be running out of bread for the queue outside his shop, but had a few loaves for those who could afford a back-hander. The perpetual circle of back-handers was in full swing.

During the summer holidays, Myra started to take an interest in cooking, to keep herself occupied. After all she was a girl, and girls should be able to cook as well as their mothers and grandmothers. But she dreaded the ritual of killing the birds. Things had changed though. Myra remembered the time when they lived with the grandparents. Esther used to take her to the ritual place on station road, where the *shochet* performed the killing of the bird. There, a man with a long beard sprinkled with red blood, wearing a long kaftan on top of which there was a once- white apron all sprinkled with blood in various stages of decomposition, first inspected the bird. Then, with a swift movement, his knife cut at the hen at the neck, severing the arteries and letting the blood flow freely. He hung the animal upside down on a hook where it pitifully struggled till its last breath.

When Esther collected the hen, it was put on a stone table outside, where she and Myra plucked it clean. All the time conversations continued between Esther and other women engaged in the same task.

When times changed the ritual was ended. Quite a nuisance, Esther complained. When Usher was out she had to ask a neighbour, or a farmer who passed by, to kill her chicken for her.

Esther cooked as generations of women had cooked before her: she rubbed the quartered chicken pieces with salt and let the remaining juices drain. While that was happening she started on the vegetables. Myra and Dolly were watching and Myra often offered to help but Esther dismissed the offer.

'Keep away. You are so clumsy.It's like you have two left hands,' she said. Dolly laughed and went outside skipping while Myra sulked.

Esther often made pastry. She spread the dough on the table, pulling gently until the whole table top was covered. She let Myra and Dolly help a little under supervision. Armed with a water glass each, the two girls were allowed to press it into the pastry and cut a round, and then another. In the middle of each, Esther put a little of the filling mixture she had prepared. The best was the filling made of potatoes and fried onion in chicken fat - called *schmaltz* - and the ones with liver and chicken cracklings and fried onions. The pastry rounds were turned over to make a half-moon shape and Esther stuck the edges together with a fork.

'Don't count them, girls,' she would say. 'If you do, the *varenikies* are bound to come undone.'

They did not count, not out loud that is. Myra waited for them to split open while they were boiling and betray her secret counting, but they never did. They always came out beautifully.

When lunch was served it looked so lovely: the red beetroot borscht, served with the golden *varenikies*, oozing with hot golden *schmaltz*.

On Fridays Esther cooked fish when she could get it: carp baked on a bed of potatoes and onions served cold on a Friday night, the juice turned to a light jelly, gefilte fish and fresh *tarama*. The girls watched her at work and Myra promised herself that one day she would cook dishes at least as good as her Mama's.

Esther had ambitions for her girls. When money started to come in, she convinced Usher that the girls would enjoy playing an instrument. One day, an upright piano was delivered. The town piano teacher, Mrs Segal, was invited to call. She was married to the man who for years ran the bookshop in Station Road and, for a time under the new rules was still allowed to keep the shop, to sell books and stationery.

Mrs Segal was a tall woman, plump in body but with very long thin legs and very fine hands with long fingers.

'Mrs Segal has hairs on her chin,, like a man,' Dolly told her father in the evening.

'And on her legs,' added Myra.

Usher did not say a thing, just carried on with his food.

'Enough of gossip,' snapped Esther. 'She is a good piano teacher. No smirking and giggling!'

The girls were now fully occupied with school work, activities with the Pioneers, French and German lessons at Mrs Kremnitzer's house and piano lessons. There was little time left for play.

Every day Usher came home from work for his lunch, covered in dust and sweat. By that time the girls were home from school, which was starting early, at 7am, and finished at 12 noon for Dolly. Once school started, she insisted she was to be called Bea, her real name. One o'clock was the time when school finished for Myra.

Usher was not allowed into the house in his working clothes, so Esther served lunch in the kitchen. He then took Esther aside and handed over the day's takings, the notes that Myra noticed bulging out of his pockets. He also left Esther the accounts to do. He must come out correct in the figures, and Esther knew how to do the books.

In the afternoon all work stopped. The girls put on nice clothes, most of them made by Esther. She herself dressed up a little and the three of them went out for a stroll on the High Street. On the days when the girls had their language lessons, she took them to old Mrs Kremnitzer.

On the way Esther kept on telling Myra, 'Keep your head up. There's no need to count the stones on the pavement.' She told Bea, 'Stop jumping and skipping. Walk properly!'

They would progress at leisurely pace along the High Street stopping, if there was time, to greet old Mrs Singer, or Mrs Stoler, who put her chair out in front of her ironmongery shop every afternoon. The shop was now manned by her son. Or they would call at Jenny's boutique. Jenny and her husband Dan were related to Usher. Their shop was lovely, full of ribbons and pins with decorated mannequin heads and gloves and scarves.

Esther could not resist telling everyone who was there to listen, how clever her girls were, how well they were doing at school. Greetings, kisses and news were exchanged.

When the language lessons were over, Esther came to collect the girls and the walk along the High Street continued. Before going home, Esther would make a detour, something the girls eagerly awaited. She took them to visit the ice cream parlour in Mr Nitzescu's garden. Ever since his patisserie was closed by the authorities, he made ice cream at home and served it to a few people he knew. He made chocolate ice cream, cassata, sorbets.

In the summer they sat in the garden and chatted with Mr and Mrs Nitzescu about old times, the cakes he used to make, the new taxes, the inspections from the police. On Sundays, when Usher joined them, they went to the public gardens to sit on the green-painted benches and see what new flower- beds the gardener had put on display that season.

It was a lovely garden, with paths covered in shingle and sand, plants and flower bushes artistically set in round or square shapes.

The perfume of linden and horse chestnut blossom mingled with jasmine, tobacco flowers and stocks in a riot of colours and smells.

There is no doubt the family was living better. Every three months Getta, the washerwoman, came to help Esther with the laundry. Sheets, pillow cases, towels, shirts and dresses were gathered together. Much of the bedding formed part of Esther's dowry, so long ago now, but still with the delicate broderie anglaise she had spent her youth embroidering. This was a big wash, and Getta was booked to work for three whole days.

A fire was built in the yard and a big copper cauldron full of water was set up on supports above the fire. The water boiled gently while the laundry had soaked overnight in cold water mixed with soap and a handful of caustic soda in a wooden tub.

Getta squeezed and wrung each item, then put it into the boiling water. The smells of suds, soap and burning wood filled the air. Esther had already sorted items by colour and fibre. She was happy: at least she no longer needed to make the soap as her mother used to.

Getta kept turning the hot water and pounded them with a wooden long piece. Then she took the laundry out, piece by piece squeezing and wringing again. and dropped it back into the wooden tub She looked exhausted, her small frame even smaller and her wrinkled, weather-beaten face darker.

The laundry was left in cold water until the next morning with a touch of blue added to the water to make the whites even whiter. Esther thought of the time she used to do this job herself with her mother, for her father and four brothers and reminded the girls that life was not easy.

Usher came home and paid Getta for her day's work. He knew that tomorrow he would have a job to find her.His prediction proved true. Esther was furious. Getta had not shown up the following morning. Usher took his bicycle and went searching on street corners, on pavements and in doorways. At last he found her fast asleep in front of her own little house. She had almost made it home, drunk as she was. That was her failing: once she was washerwoman, employed in the best houses by rich landlords and well-to-do families, but the drink made her sink lower and lower.

There was nothing to do but help her indoors and let her sleep it off. Esther and Usher hung out the washing to dry.

There was almost perfect division of labour in the household. Usher went to the market each Sunday without fail, buying fruit and vegetables, depending on the season. He went on his bike several times. The last journey he made was to fetch the ice from the ice factory, which was in the middle of the covered market. He brought home the large block of ice on his bike, and the ice went into the box in the cellar.

Then he went to fetch the chicken and other meat put aside for him by the butcher. Sometimes he got a lamb, or half a lamb, from his clients who came from the villages. Esther did the cooking. She cooked enough for a whole week, different dishes that would keep and only need to be reheated.

During the summer Usher went somewhere in the country to order firewood for the winter. The wood arrived in large logs which sometimes he had to cut to size himself and sometimes got someone to help. He stored the wood in the shed in carefully planned rows.

Later on, charcoal was on sale but nobody liked it. It made too much smoke and it did not suit the large terra-cotta brick stoves. It gave people headaches. In the late sixties Esther would achieve her dream of an electric hob with two rings to cook on..

Drinking water came from a tap outside, until Usher managed to extend a pipe into the kitchen. There was no bathroom in the house. When they were young, the children bathed in a zinc tub in the kitchen, filled with water that was boiled in large kettles. Once a week the grown-ups went to the communal baths, where Myra and Bea joined their parents when they grew old enough.

Bathers had to book in advance for the days reserved for women or those reserved for men. Once inside, undressed to their birthday suits, they entered a large room full of steam. The room was lined with stone steps climbing higher and higher, like a Roman amphitheatre. It was hard to see anything until the eyes adjusted to the thick mist.

In the middle of the room there was a square basin full of water. Cold water, as Myra discovered when she jumped in; it took her breath away.

All around the sound of women could be heard, their talking and the rhythmic sound of the brooms with which they were beating their naked flesh. The heat and the choking steam were overwhelming and from time to time Esther had to take the girls out to recover.

When they grew richer they could afford to book an individual tub by the hour. One by one Esther would wash their hair and soap and rinse their backs before taking her turn.

15
THE AWAKENING

Another summer was showing signs of ending with the leaves turning yellow and the air more mellow. Esther started thinking of the next school term. Bea had grown such a lot that she could almost wear Myra's uniform dress of two years ago, although there were nearly seven years between them.

Esther looked at Myra, her eyes travelling up and down, and she sighed.

'You've grown, Myra. Not much, but you have grown. Let's try last term's dress on.'

'It's a little short, a little tight, Mama'.

'You are growing the wrong way girl!' Esther said with a frown.

In the wrong again. The old feeling of guilt returned, but Myra wasn't quite sure what she was guilty of. She understood that her mother meant she was getting plump. Or that she had noticed her budding breasts.

She hoped Esther has not noticed her bosom. Myra bent forward so it didn't stick out too much. She did that at school a lot, so the other girls would stop laughing and pointing at her breasts.

Most of her school friends were taller and their chests were flat. They called her names: 'Dumpling' and 'Doughnut' were the most common. She laughed so that she did not cry. She had noticed that if she was upset the girls tormented her more.

At least the teachers liked her. She was the best in her class at all subjects except singing and sports. She had a nice, clear speaking voice and could be relied on to recite long poems at the school fete.

'Mama, I can't go to school in this dress. The other girls will laugh at me. I've told you what they're like.'

'I can't see why,' says Esther. 'It's all in your mind. Anyway, I have no time to sort that out.'

Dismissed again, Myra thought. She remembered the last term's end of the year celebration. Esther had sent her to school in a red dress that she had made for her a couple of years previously. It was a nice dress- Tyrolese, she called it. The skirt was short and the waist was high, and the thin silky material of the blouse allowed her breasts to show. The girls pointed at her, giggling, and some of them even dared to pinch her nipples.

16
SISTERLY LOVE

In the early fifties, polio was the most dreaded illness, feared by parents and children alike. Some of Myra's school friends were hit. Some went into the hospital, and when they came out, if they ever did, their limbs had turned useless, like jelly.

Soon after the time that Bea started school, her friend Sylvia was admitted to the local hospital, with suspected polio.She came out months later stuck in a large pram. She was kept in that pram for the rest of her life. The primary school was very near their home and Bea went out in the morning with Myra, but preferred to come home on her own, to prove she was grown up.

Bea was a proper tomboy and she had lots of falls. Esther spent a lot of time comforting her, cleaning up grazes and putting on plasters. Each time Myra came home from her school, she would find Esther and Bea together.

But that early afternoon, Myra came home to find the house empty.

'Mama, I am home!' There was no answer.

'I wonder where they've gone,' Myra muttered to herself, thinking Bea must have long been home from her school. The doors were open, that meant that they could not be far. Myra changed her school uniform, put on a dress, took a book out of her bag and started reading.

Time passed and Myra began to feel hungry. How strange, she noticed there was no hot food prepared, no pots or pans on the stove. So unlike her mother. She went to the bread bin and tore a slice from the bread left from yesterday .She took it out to eat, careful not to fill the kitchen with crumbs, not to give Esther a chance to scream at her again and went back to her book. It was getting late and there was no sign of anyone. Myra got up, closed the gate carefully and started walking. It was not far to the timber yard where Usher was working. She reached the place, only to find the heavy gates shut. There was no one in sight to ask. Myra got frightened. Where were they all? Where had they gone without telling her?

Myra ran back towards home. An elderly lady who kept a little knitting shop on the main road came out of her house and stopped Myra.

'How is your sister?' she asked, 'Is she all right?'

Myra looked at her bewildered. 'What happened, was my sister hurt?'

'Oh, I don't know,' she said. 'Your sister took a fall on the street just here and she could not get up, she ...never mind, someone ran to get your mother and I went quickly to tell your father and they both came and took her. They all left in a carriage, that's all I know.'

Stunned, Myra returned slowly home trembling not knowing what to do next. Where should she go? Where could she find her family?

The neighbours, Janna's parents, had not seen nor heard a thing. She decided to stay put. The lovely book she was reading no longer made sense.

It was dark when Usher returned. He looked haggard and frightened.

'What happened, Daddy?'

'Bea is ill, the doctors said she may have polio.'

Oh, is she going to be crippled ? Like Sylvia? Where is Mama?'

'She stayed in the hospital, the doctors let her sleep in a chair outside our little Dolly's room,' he said and started to cry. 'She could not leave her.'

'Can I go to see them?'

'No, you cannot! They are in the isolation ward. You'd better take care of the house now.'

'When will we know for sure?' Myra asked, by now crying herself as well.

'Please God, tomorrow. They are going to put a needle in Dolly's back, get a little juice to see if it is polio.'

'Like Sylvia from school, who cannot walk anymore?'

'Shut up, I do not want to hear this!' Usher said, covering his ears.

He started sobbing loudly. Myra was frightened as he kneeled on the kitchen floor and put his hands together in prayer.

'Please God, hear my voice, save my child, save my hope!'

Myra was surprised; she never thought her father would pray to God. He who did not believe and dismissed religion! She still remembered the row he had had with the grandparents when he brought home the first radio set they had ever seen. It was a Friday night when Grandpa and Grandma had started screaming, saying that they would not have that infernal machine in their home and they had called Daddy a GOY! Esther had screamed and hollered at her parents and her mother had slapped her face. The next day they moved   out.

Night passed without incident but Myra took a long time to fall asleep. Images passed through her mind; Bea starting school, tall for her age and thin and full of life. She already knew how to read and write. Myra herself had taught her. Bea did not know what hardship meant. She had grown up knowing only that life was good, all she had to do was to ask for things and they would be given. She got her two wheeler bike when she was three, and Myra taught her to ride, then she had a pair of skates. They spent long hours together. Myra played teacher and Bea was the pupil. That worked well till Bea felt she knew everything and started to contradict Myra and stamped her little foot. How they started arguing! And Bea cried and run to Mama, and Esther shouted at Myra, 'Myra, leave Dolly alone, don't upset her, let her win!'

'But Mama, this is not right, she cannot do this!'

'Never you mind, just let her have her way, can't you see how upset she gets? You are old enough to know better.'

Dolly had her own way and after all that, when Usher was back from work, she was the first to greet him and start to tell him how Myra shouted at her and did not let her touch her things and all her long list of complaints.

Myra smiled now, remembering all those scenes, which no longer mattered. All she wanted was to see her Dolly back home healthy and safe.

Next morning Usher left early. Myra did not go to school. She tidied the beds and made an attempt to clean the kitchen. It was not easy, there were too many small carpets and corners to sweep. She washed the few dishes left from the previous night in cold water, dried them and put them in the cupboard. She tried her best to do what her mother would do. She kept thinking of Bea, her Dolly, how much pain she might be suffering and she thought of her mother's tears and her father's last night's sorrow.

Myra did not know what to cook. She had never had to cook . She was never allowed to do anything in the kitchen. Mamma long ago, declared Myra had clumsy hands. She found potatoes and peeled them and a few onions. She went out to buy bread. She was going to tell the baker to credit her till her father came home. There was some cheese and butter in the cold store, but no milk. She came home, made a sandwich for herself and prepared one for her father, in case he returned for lunch. He came back to say the test was performed and now they had to wait for the result. He was not allowed to see Dolly, but the doctor was confident and he trusted old Doctor Diaconescu: there would be good news .He gratefully ate his sandwich and fried some of the potatoes which they both shared. Usher could not settle. Myra could hear him pacing the floor, then he went out again. He came back very late and went straight to bed. The morning came and at lunch time Usher, Esther and Dolly walked in, all smiles.

'Mama,' Myra said, moving to embrace her mother, but Esther gave her only a limp embrace. She was looking tired and hastened to put Bea to bed.

After a while, she came back to the kitchen and went to the stove, put her spectacles on and prepared to start making something for lunch.

'What is this mess? All these oil stains!' she exclaimed. 'I couldn't leave you two a single moment,'she said addressing Usher and Myra.

'Leave it now.' Usher looked upset. Myra did not say a thing, silently cursing herself for having forgotten to wipe the stove clean of the frying oil.

Bea recovered but on and off that year had a few more faints. One day, the next door neighbour, Mrs Herscovitz, had a visit from her son. He was a well-known paediatrician in the capital. Usher and Esther took Bea for a consultation and with his treatment Dolly never had those turns again. It did not stop Bea from playing up and demanding even more attention than before.

It was a relief to break up for the summer, even if there was not much to do at home. It would have been nice to cry on someone's shoulder, but there was no shoulder to cry on. Esther was busy.

Bea was just a child and needed all Mama's attention. Esther had to supervise her at home, to make sure she ate properly after her serious illness.

Usher was a man and one could not speak of such things to him; he would not understand. Besides he was always in a hurry, covered in dust and so tired that he fell asleep at the least opportunity.

It occurred to Myra that she would talk to Mrs Neubauer, the geography teacher. She was such a nice lady, who always treated Myra like a grown-up. She praised her and encouraged her reading. Mrs Neubauer had said on several occasions that during the holidays Myra could visit her at home and borrow books.

17
GROWING UP

Myra went and she was invited to tea and cake with Mrs Neubauer and her mother, while Mr Neubauer tended their large garden. He was a large man with rust coloured hair and a beard and did not say much. Mrs Neubower talked about school, and helped Myra chose a book on the promise that she will come again and tell her all about it.

Nobody knew where that family came from, even in that small town, where people knew practically everyone and everything about each other. Their name was German and they were most likely from Transylvania, where most Romanian Germans lived. After the war some important people were exiled to live in Focsani. The little town was full of ex-university teachers, renowned physicians and lawyers who had been demoted from the important positions they held before the republic The people accepted them, nobody knew or cared why they were there.

Myra met Marianna, a new friend she had made just before the end of the last school term. She was a lovely girl with large blue eyes and golden hair. Marianna invited Myra to her house. For once, she didn't encounter any opposition from her parents who were too busy with the most recent events. Marianna lived with her mother. There was no father and Marianna did not talk about him, and

Myra never asked. But the girls liked each other from the start.

Myra was invited to tea. Mother and daughter lived near the Post Office, opposite the High School for Girls Al. I. Cuza, in two rented rooms at the back of a large house.

The mother greeted Myra with open arms. 'I am so pleased Marianna has found a friend at her new school.'

She looked like a grown-up copy of her daughter; she smiled and was full of cuddles and kisses. At first Myra was a little bewildered by the close contact, but soon began to enjoy the warm hugs.

The mother sat with the girls, played cards with them and told them stories of faraway towns, plays she had seen and churches she had visited in her youth. She showed them her album of photos of famous film stars. Her memories were fascinating.

There were moments when Myra looked at mother and daughter, the mother's arms round her daughter's shoulders, their heads almost touching, and thought wistfully of what her Mama often said, that a child should be kissed only when he or she were asleep. Usher felt differently. He liked to cuddle and let the girls play with his curly hair, even letting them tie ribbons in it. But he was seldom at home; always working.

'You can ask my mum any question you want and she will answer,' Marianna told Myra. So, one afternoon, the girls made up their minds to overcome their shyness and ask some questions they felt Myra could not ask at home or at school. Nowhere. It was forbidden to talk about those things. It was taboo. There were just whispers, some exciting, some frightening.

That day Marianna's mother did not answer the way Esther had: 'The stork brought them.' Why did she think that Myra was such a fool? She knew Mama had carried Bea in the swelling tummy she tried to keep hidden under her clothes, and had given birth to her in the night in the grandparents' house.

But how did the baby get there?

Esther dismissed such questions, and the more she refused to answer, the more preoccupied Myra was with the question. Sometimes she could get a hint from the books she read, the grown-up books she borrowed from her beloved geography teacher.

'Oh, something happens between a man and a woman,' the two friends whispered to each other.

Marianna's mother did not answer the girls' questions straight away. First she went out of the room. She came back after a few minutes with an old book, the pages dog-eared and yellow with age. It was called, 'How to Please Your Husband'. 'The secret of a successful marriage,' was printed underneath in smaller letters.

She opened the book at a page where a drawing labelled 'the female genitalia' was displayed. On the next page there was a diagram of 'the male genitalia'.

The girls covered their eyes in shock, then started to look through their splayed fingers and read. At the sentence, 'A man's organ penetrates the woman's private parts,' they started giggling uncontrollably.

It took a long time for their mirth to subside.

'But, Mum,' Marianna asked, 'How does it stay in there?'

'It get hard and stays up, and has a wonderful fluid inside, which carries the seed of life.'

'How big is it?' asked Myra, horrified at the prospect.

'Like, say, half a baguette.'

'Ouch. That must hurt.'

The girls giggled again, but were a bit scared.

They left it at that and went out to play. Marianna's mother smiled.

On her way home, what she had just learned would not leave Myra's mind. She went over it again and again, the same fragment of information. She was 11, almost 12. Would that have to happen to her?

She arrived home still thinking.

Tea was ready and they sat together round the table.

'Daydreaming again,' said her mother. 'Don't eat so much. Look at your thighs. They have doubled in size lately.'

Myra did not say a word, but instinctively pulled down her short dress to cover her knees.

She can talk, she thought. Mama was growing stout like a pudding too.

115

Myra's day dream returned to what she had learned of the 'facts of life'.

Night time falls in layers of shadows. Myra is reading. The light of a small pocket torch is shed on the bed covers under which she is reading and is reflected back onto the book. 'Gone with the Wind'. What a magnificent book. Myra imagines herself Scarlett O'Hara. What a strong woman. She would love to be like her.

The silence of the night is suddenly disturbed. A thin glass door separates her room from her parents' room. She closes the book, switches off the torch and listens intently. Something seems to be happening in the next room.

Her parents are doing it, she thinks. Her father is moaning and groaning. She thinks she can hear her mother whispering from time to time, 'Enough, enough.' Yuck! How revolting!

Myra thought of the white rubber things in her mother's bedside table that she spotted the other day. She even blew one up. It looked just like a balloon. She thought to inflate them all, tie them up and leave them round the house, just to show them she knew, just to see their faces. But she thought better of it. It was too dangerous. She was bound to be severely punished. It was not worth it.

Myra was struggling to finish her homework. She was finding it hard to keep her mind on her lessons. She still went once a week to Mrs Kremnitzer for her private lessons in French and

German. The lady mentioned that Myra's homework had deteriorated.

One sunny afternoon Myra was returning home from her language lesson. The air was still and heavy and Myra dragged her feet in a slow walk. She was not eager to be at home just yet.

Then she passed a shop doorway and she remembered the shoemaker and stopped.

The door was open and the shop was dark inside.

She remembered that Daddy had said that she should call at the shop to be measured for new shoes. Then she heard a man's voice coming from the darkness.

'Hello Myra. How are you? Do come in.'

Myra could not see in the dark and advanced cautiously, trying to avoid the benches and tools and trying not to trip over anything.. The shoemaker's shape materialised in the gloom. He smiled and his eyes narrowed in a friendly welcome. Myra recognised his bent back, almost like a big question mark. She recognised the bald head on the top, with a few strands of hair falling over his ears, the large glasses on the tip of his nose. He was one of Daddy's friends.

Still smiling, he looked her up and down, and suddenly Myra felt uneasy. She became aware of her short dress. But Mamma had said that she was still a child and it would do. She should have left then and there ,but he held her hand tight and she followed him in.

'Daddy said will you measure my feet, please. He will come to settle the bill later.'

The shoemaker pointed to a little stool with several markings of soles showing patterns and numbers from small to large sizes and he guided her there. He put a sheet of card on top of the stool and took a pencil from behind his ear. He asked Myra to put her right foot on the card.

He came from behind and bent over her. His right hand reached down to adjust the position of her foot. Myra could smell his sour breath with a hint of garlic.

With the same hand he started drawing with the pencil the outline of her foot. With his other hand he touched the inside of her leg.

Myra tried to put her foot down, but he held her tight. She felt his left hand rising up on her tigh to the edge of her pants. She was frightened and pulled her foot away.

'Stay. I have to take the shape of your other foot,' he said. 'What will your parents say if I tell them you wouldn't keep still, so I couldn't measure you? Come on. I won't do anything to you.'

Myra remained rooted to the spot. All her strength and power of reasoning had left her. The shoemaker grabbed her hand and obediently she put her left foot on the stool.

Again the shoemaker started drawing with his right hand. Myra could feel the tip of his pencil tickling her toes. His left hand touched her bottom and she felt his fingernail scratching the elastic of her pants. He slowly parted the material from her skin and advanced towards her most intimate parts. He parted the lips, and his fingers felt like hot iron. She started to whimper.

'Oh, hello. I thought there was nobody here,' a man's voice called from the front door.

The shoemaker released his grip. Myra put her foot down and hurried, groping towards the daylight. She did not turn round. She ran and ran, and the burning ran with her.

She reached home, rushed to the toilet and locked the door. She checked her pants. Nothing. No blood. She was sure she was injured. As soon as she could she would find a mirror to make sure.

She hoped nobody would know what happened. It would stay buried in her being, like so many other secrets.

She went into the house and found a book and her homework. Esther lifted her eyes from the book-keeping ledger she was working on for Usher. She was content to see Myra doing her work without being prompted.

From next door came discordant sounds; Bea was trying her hand at the piano

.

Myra decided she would never go to that shop again, or go into any other place by herself. Her nights were haunted by terror. The tree in front of her window, the changing colours of which she used to love through the seasons of the year, was turning into a nightmarish monster. The branches swaying in the wind came through the glass and she was convinced they were reaching out to touch her. She was frightened to stay awake or to fall asleep. She was very tired.

Esther took her to see the children's doctor. He said Myra was growing up and prescribed her a tonic. He reassured Esther that Myra would grow out of these moods.

Myra no longer visited Marianna. She had somehow lost interest. The whole subject of love between men and women seemed disgusting. In future she will be wary of any man and avoid any contact with them. She felt it was better to try to forget about what happened., but the nights were still difficult.

When she started at the senior school, with new teachers and new students, the memory of what happened receded into the deepest folds of her consciousness and became part of her lost childhood. But it never disappeared completely. It came lurching back from time to time, prompted by new encounters.

18
ANCA

She noticed the girl as they were standing at the first class assembly. She was at least one head above the other girls, with large sad eyes. Her face was delicately chiselled, a small turned up nose and almost olive skin. Her hair, cut short, was an array of curls. It was impossible to say what attracted Myra, perhaps the girl's aloofness, her isolation in her own impenetrable space, but she could not take her eyes off her. On the following school days, Myra arrived at school eager to seek that fascinating girl. And when one day they arrived at school at the same time, they smiled and started talking. It did not take long for Myra and Anca to become inseparable. Anca spoke with a quiet, well-mannered voice. Myra spoke loudly, trying to impress. Anca was tall and slender, Myra was small and plump. Anca did everything quietly and precisely while Myra was untidy and clumsy. The instant they met, Anca assumed the role of looking after and protecting Myra. When school was over they found it hard to part. They thought almost the same thoughts and laughed at the same things. They read the same books and discussed them at length.

Myra spent most afternoons with Anca. They learned to play some Strauss waltzes four handed at the piano. The synchronisation was a little faulty and the waltz changed into a stop-start quick-step. Poor Mrs Boiou, Anca's mother, had to cover her ears, but the girls laughed, and in the end she laughed with them.

Almost every time, the visit ended at Anca's home or at Anca's aunt's, next door, where tea was served: lemon tea in fine china cups with home-baked teacakes. They talked about books, about philosophy – Kant, Laplace, Confucius, Schopenhauer. Anca's aunt was such an interesting woman, tall and still handsome, with a graceful way of moving. In her old-fashioned clothes, she wore an air of melancholy which moved with her without a sound.

Her husband, once a powerful landowner, had returned from prison a spent man. He was much older than his wife and his years in prison under the communists had devastated his later life. He walked with bent knees, his back bent in a hump, and he was so thin his clothes hung on him as if on a scarecrow. He looked like a man who had lost everything.

Anca and Myra would quickly finish their homework, then start to enjoy themselves. They went for walks and painted, even built a house for the cat.

One day Anca had the grand idea of performing a surgical operation. Since they both wanted to study medicine, Anca reasoned they should start early. At first she considered the cat but Myra objected, arguing that since they did not have anaesthetic it would inflict too much pain on the poor cat – she remembered how painful it felt after her appendix was taken out.

So they settled on a frog they found on the bank of the brook running behind the garden, although neither of them knew if a frog had an appendix or not. Anca found a pair of nail scissors, some forceps from her mother's cabinet, some white cotton and a needle. Anca washed her hands while Myra dutifully poured some surgical spirit into a dish, lit it with a match and sterilised the instruments.

With the scissors Anca made an incision in the frog's abdomen while Myra struggled to keep it still. The insides of the frog spilled out. No appendix was found. Myra was instructed to close the wound and suture the skin. She did it with great care, but the frog was no longer aware of what was happening for she had expired during the procedure.

They were such children, Myra thought years later. At 13 and 14 they played like much younger children. Imagine nowadays a 14-year-old playing a game of pretend surgeons. Or playing four hands at the piano, or writing poetry one line each, without the other reading the previous line, and giggling over the result.

There was no television or portable telephone then. The radio dished out programs about the communist party and its teachings. Gatherings of young people were forbidden. There was very little to do in the long hot summers. More friends joined the group: Ony, Antoinetta, Georgetta. Christina. They were the top achievers at school, the elite.

A swimming pool opened in the town and the group of five girls started going occasionally, mostly when there were few other people there, particularly avoiding the boys from the Union Lyceum, the senior school for boys.

19
LOG RAFTS ON THE
RIVER BISTRITZA

Myra was about 14 years old and Bea 5 when Esther took them for a holiday to a spa famous for its natural mineral waters and the healthy mountain air. Vatra Dorney was situated in western Bucovina, in the north-west of Romania. The beautiful fast river of Bistritza ran through it. Esther had promised that if the weather was good she would take the girls and go rafting on the river. 'There was a long tradition in that part of the country to transport logs from the mountains forests on the river. Myra learned at school about this and was eager to impart her knowledge with her sister and mother. 'This was a way of life for the riverine villagers and the profession was passed from father to son,' she cited from the large pool of memory.

On that August day Esther kept her word; she was as eager as the girls to go. They climbed on the large log raft, struggling to keep their balance. A boy, about Myra's age stood with his legs apart, as if they were growing out of the wood at the fore edge of the raft handling a very long oar. The sun was shinning bright, the light filtered through the dense foliage of the forest which framed each side of the bank. The great frothing river was almost covered by the large rafts, some lying idle, stuck in the bays of the river bank, some being driven, some moving along with the strong current. The logs on the raft were tied tight to each other, not a drop of water slipped in between. Esther looked for a place to sit but soon realised that there was nowhere except then lie down on the raft. She set the example and went flat on her back, her face up to the sky. Myra and Bea followed and the three of them remained there for a long time, relaxed and happy, watching the immense sky. Myra's hand trailed through the icy watter. Her eyes turned to the boy who stood upright at the front handling the oar skillfully and effortlessly, while an older man, his father, manned the back of the long raft, chewing tabacco and coughing and spitting a thick cough. Myra turned on a side hoping that she would make eye contact with the boy, but he ignored her. However there was a slight change in his posture. He pushed his hat even lower over his eyes and pushed his chest out.

Suddenly Bea sat up and shouted with delight: look Mama, there is silver fish in the air. Myra lifted her head and Bea was right; silver fish somer-saulted in and out of the water near the bank. 'Flying trout,' the older man said, and he took out a rod and set out fishing, leaving all the heavy punting to the boy.

It was a long journey for the raft, it carried logs all the way down the river to Bacau for the paper factory, the man told them. It was too long for Bea to keep still and she started walking trying to balance on a single log, one step in front of the other. As expected, she soon lost her balance and had a fall. But Mama remained where she was, watching the sky, deep in her thoughts.

20
SKELETONS IN CUPBOARDS

Invitations to join the Union of Socialist Youth made the girls uneasy. Membership was no simple matter. It meant lots of meetings and declaring allegiance to communism. It meant that one had to betray parents and family. Every family had its own secrets. There were calls to attend meetings, parades and voluntary work. It was all boring and time-consuming.

More worrying was that before becoming a member of the organisation everyone had to write a detailed account of the background of their family members, their attitude towards the teachings of the Party, the way they applied the prescribed teachings of the Party at work and at home, and whether they had any relatives living in the capitalist West.

Most of the students Myra knew who were her friends had their baggage of problems. Ony's father had been detained in prison for a few years because he had been a prominent judge before the war. Anca's family had been practically destroyed; her uncle, one of the richest landowners was brought to the state of a beggar and her aunt ill with depression because of her sufferings at the hands of the Russian soldiers. Anca's father had been sent to a distant hospital to work and her mother practised as a dental surgeon until one day in 1954 small businesses were nationalised by decree and she had lost her dental surgery overnight.

Myra herself was not whiter than white. She would have to confess that she had relatives living abroad, practically a whole family of grandparents and uncles. Because her mother refused to make contact with her brothers, Myra had taken it upon herself to keep a correspondence going with Uncle Abraham in Israel.

Myra and Anca never spoke to each other about these problems, but without word the girls decided to give the Union of Socialist Youth a miss, keeping their heads down if they could, not filling in the form and when asked why not, saying they had forgotten, or that there was no time because of pressure of work. They would apply as soon as they could.

They finally graduated a year early. The education system was reduced by one year, to match the system in the Soviet Union. The option was to take two classes in one year and prepare for the universities' entrance examination.

Anca said from the start that she wanted to study Medicine. Myra wanted to study chemistry, to become a biochemist. She changed her mind after Usher took her one day to visit a factory specialising in beauty products and perfumes. The overwhelming pungent smell and the noise of the machinery put her off.

Besides, Myra wanted to be with Anca, and Anca wanted the two of them to stay together and study together. So they started private lessons with Mrs Margalit, their biology teacher. It was hard work but the thought of starting a new life, meeting new people and becoming someone who was respected in the community drew the girls on. They revised together with Christina and Liliana, who wanted to apply to medical school as well and, for once Esther did not object to the friendship between Myra and Anca, which she had always regarded with suspicion.

And they got in!

Soon afterwards, in September 1955, Bunica Anna, Usher's mother, came bringing news that Aunt Clara and Clara's husband Iszu had papers to emigrate to Israel.

It was a joy to see her again. Myra remembered her, a tiny woman, skinny, her face lined and wrinkled more by the hard life she had led than by her age. She was a kind, simple woman.

Myra remembered her Aunt Clara as the beautiful woman with long black wavy hair, her mouth full of pins, sticking them one by one into the garment on her lap. Their house was always full of smoke from the cigarettes. Bunica Anna smoked. She remembered the thick fog in which tiny threads danced, all colours, transparent and sparkling in the sun streaming through the windows.

Bunica Anna came to stay for a few weeks with Esther, Usher and the grandchildren, having left Clara to settle their affairs. Myra spent hours talking to her, telling how she had sat her entrance exams: anatomy, literature and language, maths, Russian, history of the socialist revolution. And she had passed, just by the skin of her teeth, with the lowest permissible mark. But she was in! Then

130

she told her about Anca, and how happy she was to go to university together.

Bunica Anna smiled her happy smile and was pleased for her. Bea had never met Bunica Anna before and she sat quietly listening to the old lady, observing her every move.

The day came when Esther, Usher and the children went with Bunica to the train station, where she was due to meet Clara to travel on to Bucharest and then to leave the country. The train steamed in and Aunt Clara could be seen in the distance, her head and shoulders out of the compartment window, waving frantically, her long black hair flowing in the wind. Beside her was a man with short wavy hair, a gaunt face and a long nose. He smiled and waved. A gold tooth in the front could be seen sparkling in the sun. 'That must be Iszu,' Myra told Bea. 'Clara's husband.'

The goodbyes and tears and hugs and kisses went on as long as the train was stopped. Esther was not crying. She was simply relieved when it was all over. She was never inclined to emotional displays particularly in a public place. Usher buried his head on his mother's shoulder and wept .They spent a long time together. Bunica, Clara and Iszou left and nobody mentioned Gutzu. Most likely he was left where he had sat, mumbling and staring into space. Myra never asked. She was too full of her new life, looking forward to university, to spare a thought for Gutzu either.

October brought trepidation and great changes. Old friends said goodbye and promised to keep in touch, to write often. Liliana went to Timishoara to study nursing, as she hadn't passed the entrance exam for Med School. Christina stayed at home to look after her younger sisters and brothers. Ony went to Bucharest to study architecture. Geta went to Yashi to study engineering. Antoaneta married as soon as school was over; like her mother, she married a much older man.

Myra hoped to get a place in student accommodation on the university campus but Esther and Usher would not hear of it. 'Heaven knows what filthy habits she would acquire.' Instead she was placed in the care of some distant cousins of Esther's, who lived in Bucharest.

21
THE STUDENT YEARS

She began her 'independent living' in Bucharest. Myra lodged with Anna and Yasha Peremisler. They lived in an elegant, small block of flats previously owned by a rich old lady who had lost her fortune, first to the fascists before the war, then again after the war when the post-war socialist order nationalised all large properties. She was reduced to a small apartment in the building, which she shared with her son. Anna had moved into the elegant three-storey block in the early 1930s, just after it was built.

The Peremislers' place was a semi-basement flat that is half under- and half over-ground, with light coming in from narrow windows set in the top part of the rooms, through which one could see the legs and shoes and baskets of people passing by, but never the people to whom they belonged. The apartment consisted of a small entrance hall and two rooms joined by glass doors. The first of these rooms was Myra's. To her this cramped and dimly lit space was freedom, away from her strict parents.

The couple had no children of their own. They were under instructions from Myra's parents to report to them any deviation from the path of learning, any parties that she attended, anything they considered frivolous. For her part, Myra had no wild plans. It was all new to her. She was just happy to be away from home.

There was a telephone in the house and Myra's parents phoned every week for news. Myra could picture the two of them and Bea, dressed for going out, at the Post Office, where the telephonist booked the call. All three would be sitting upright, full of tension, waiting to be called to the booth to make their call.

First Myra had to answer and give a brief report of her week. So many things would have happened in the previous seven days, but on the spur of the moment nothing came to mind. So banalities were exchanged: How are you? I miss you all. I am healthy. I am eating properly. And so on.

Then Anna had to give her report. She was more worldly and knew how to speak to them and allay their fears. Myra was behaving well. There were no problems. And so the call would end.

Anna was a woman in her 40s or 50s – it was hard to tell because she had a young face and a lovely smile. She wore her grey hair in a young style, cut in a short bob. She was much younger than her husband, who had been retired for a long time. Lacking an occupation, he took it upon himself to act as administrator for the whole building.

He was the ugliest man Myra had ever seen, wrinkled, with protruding teeth, one of them shining silver. He had a sly look and a wicked smile. He spoke Romanian with a heavy Russian accent. He had come to Bucharest from Bessarabia after the First World War. Myra could not imagine how Anna could have married such a man. But he was kind to his wife and spoiled her like a daughter.

Anna worked in the Grand Store Lafayette, now a state-owned concern, nationalised by the government. While his wife was at work, Yasha busied himself cleaning the cooking pots, first wiping them with newspaper to remove the grease because there was no detergent, and no hot water during the day. When that job was done, he applied himself to cutting sheets of newspaper into small squares and stringing them up in the lavatory for use as toilet paper. Such 'luxury goods' were not available in the shops at that time. Newspapers were cheap and full of communist slogans. They were impossible to read, so people found better uses for them. With these tasks and the hours spent queuing for food, Yasha was fully occupied.

As administrator of the flats, Yasha fought a never-ending battle with the all-powerful Madam Barbara. She was the caretaker of the building and had been since it was built. It was rumoured that she reported every movement by the residents to the police, their comings and goings, their meetings, if and when they listened to forbidden western radio stations. She was treated with respect and caution, even by the old proprietor and her son.

Myra was supremely happy. She was free. Whenever she wanted, she could go and see Anca, and she was on friendly terms with Anna. Her cooking was good and she was out of the house most of the day, so she did not have to spend much time in Yasha's company.

She fell in love with the beautiful building where she lived, with its marble surround and entrance steps, the elegant wooden front doors and the large entrance hall with the lift, lined with mirrors, encased in its iron frame. Polished stone steps led past the lift down to the Peremislers' flat. Opposite their front door was the entrance to the old servants' quarters, now occupied by Madam Barbara and her daughter, and another couple who were allocated space there.

Each morning Myra took the tramcar from Matei Basarab to Union Place, then the tramcar turned right, passing the Coltzea Hospital on the way to the Centre crossroads, near the University. Then she walked along the old Elisabeth Boulevard, passing the Cishmigiou Park, the Kogalniceanou Statue, the Law School and the Opera House until she reached the Cotroceni area and the extensive grounds of the medical school. When the weather was bad she took the tramcar to the Cotroceni Palace, the former residence of the King, now converted into the Pioneers' Palace for the communist youth organisation.

The Medical School was an imposing 19th century building in the Regency style. Each day Myra passed the Porter's Lodge, she was reminded of where she sat with Esther, gripping her mother's hand tight, waiting for the entrance exam results. She had said: 'Mama, if I don't get in I cannot see my life continuing.' Esther was really worried, and for the first time she had talked to

Myra, reassuring her, telling her that she was young and could always try again the next year. Mother and daughter were very close then.

There was a large student intake that year, almost three hundred new students, and they were divided into two courses running parallel. Each half was again divided into groups of ten students for dissection, laboratory work, joining up with other groups for lectures and exams. Myra was the youngest in her group she was just seventeen, and her mother had sent her to college in her black school uniform with a white collar and white knee-length socks, keeping her better clothes for holidays at home. Most of the other girls at lectures wore fashionable pencil skirts and nylons and looked very grown-up and intimidating.

But Myra soon made friends. There was Olga from Constanza, Lya, a tall blonde with vivid blue eyes, also from Constanza. Her parents were Greeks, long ago established in Romania. She was smart, well-dressed and inclined to flirt with any man, just to reassure herself that she was desirable. Dora was a lovely, soft-spoken blonde with black eyes. Her parents had died when she was young and she lived with her grown-up sister, who was already a doctor. Soon they were all good friends, with Lya leading the group in fashion, make-up, outings and cinema trips.

The boys were all young, tall and very clever. Except for Sabin who stood apart. Sabin, was a member of the Communist party and in charge of discipline and behaviour. Every group had such a political activist whose responsibility was to keep the students in order, report any subversive activities and prevent private friendships. Some of them only had the first four elementary classes of school education and had no aptitude or inclination for academic carriers. They were selected by the party and put through an intense course of secondary education - the workers schools - and then placed in universities and colleges.. They were given an intensive educational year and accepted as students without even taking the entrance exam. They were the product of the social class that the new regime relied on.

22
A STUDENT'S LIFE IN BUCHAREST

Memories do not seem to run smoothly, one after the other in chronological order. They pop into Myra's head at random. But the order is of no consequence, she thinks. Friendship is preserved in feelings, in fragments of events imprinted on the mind. It is so strange: so many years spent in Anca's company, and so little left after graduation. They were inseparable friends, the tall and the short, the reserved and the gregarious – although when it came to decisions, quiet Anca had the last word.

The first year at medical school was a struggle to adapt to a new life. Anca was placed in the first half of the year and Myra in the second. For the first time in four years they were apart, and it was hard for both of them. Anca lodged with an old acquaintance of her mother's. She had a room of her own near the Cishmigiu Park, and her mother gave her a Burmese kitten to keep her company.

Anca's way of starting her new life was to spend most of her time playing with her kitten or reading novels – fiction, romance, detective stories – anything she could get her hands on. She was 'making up for lost time', she said. The last thing she wanted to do was study.

The two girls met every day after classes and often went to lunch together, every week in a different canteen. The canteens were eating places where office and factory workers could have an inexpensive midday meal. They were given coupons for the purpose, but many workers chose to bring a sandwich from home and sell the coupons cheap, or simply give them away. Many students relied on these coupons for a decent meal.

Myra and Anca ate often in a basement canteen near Cinema Scala, sometimes at the School of Dentistry, and sometimes at one of many other places. Once a month they shared parcels from home – cheese and fruit from Myra's parents; cakes that Anca's mother baked. Myra had a monthly grant, and while the money lasted, they treated themselves at the best patisserie in town, films, even the opera. Together with other students they soon learned ways to get cheap seats, either queuing for hours or bribing an usher that someone knew by name. That way they sat on the gallery steps and saw Madam Butterfly, Turandot, Tosca, La Traviata, Faust and many others.

But unlike Anca, Myra was determined to apply herself to study. She spent more and more time with the other students in her group revising with them. There seemed to be no end to the things they had to learn: all the anatomical details, physiology, biochemistry, on and on. It took a while to adjust to dissection – not so much getting used to carving up a fellow human being as coping with the formaldehyde he was soaked in, which stung the eyes and produced a flood of tears.

There were no standard textbooks available, so lectures had to be attended and accurate notes taken. Eventually Myra found a second-hand copy of Gray's Anatomy in an old bookshop. Lya found an English-Romanian dictionary and painstakingly they managed to work out the text.

Difficulties started with embryology. The teachers had to conform to a new directive straight Moscow: Wirchow's Theory, *omni cellula es cellulla*, was discarded as a capitalist ploy in favour of Olga Lepeshinskaia's theory, which stated that living cells were formed from an indeterminate protein mass.

Genetics were dismissed as another imperialist ploy. 'People do not have a genetic signature,' the party dogma asserted. 'Their character and abilities were the result only of their upbringing and circumstances.' Accordingly, even children from a capitalist or bourgeois background could be reformed and purified by being sent as workers to factories or farms.

As for physiology, the whole gamut of that science started and ended with Pavlov and his reflex experiments with dogs. Of course this contradicted the Larousse Medicale Encyclopedia and Gray's Anatomy. When challenged, the professors patiently explained the old teaching, then mentioned the extraordinary progress Soviet science had made, and how this made all previous teachings out of date. What else could they do? Like everybody else, they had to follow the Party line.

Lectures in Marxism-Leninism had to be faithfully attended too, so there was plenty to keep Myra busy. The pressure increased as exam-time loomed. Subjects that a student failed in spring could be retaken in September, but a second failure meant repeating the year's course. Failure in the repeated year meant being dismissed altogether, something Myra could not contemplate. She spent many sleepless nights worrying that she could not keep up. Myra, who came to the university straight after the baccalaureate felt she had swapped her school uniform for the white coat. She felt at times like she would never be free to do what she wanted to do, when she wanted it. She felt restricted: at home her landlady was under strict instructions from the austere Esther to inform her of any 'misdemeanour' particularly any contact with the opposite sex. At home she was never allowed to mix with boys. Myra felt she lacked the skills to relate socially to her male colleagues, although the boys in her study group treated her like a good chum. Together with her girlfiends Lya and Dora, she went to the Students' Club on the south bank of the river where dance evenings were organised once a week. Myra's best friend Anca did not join them, she preferred to spend time with her cat and her romance books. In the second year all the groups were disbanded and reassembled with new members, so that the fragile new friendships would dwindle away. The ones in power discouraged friendship and groups forming. A new girl joined her group and two new boys. They became great friends Aurora, Myra, Andrei and Puiu. Together on Sundays, they visited churches and old buildings, museums and with little money bought vinyl records. They sat for hours into the night listening to music, talking philosophy, politics and art. Secretly Myra felt very attracted to Puiu but there was no sign on his part that he shared her feelings and she never said anything. In a way she had felt relieved that there was no romantic involvement, she would not have known how to behave and it would have spoiled a beautiful camaraderie. They were all very short of money but it did not matter that much. They would go to a coffee shop and order a single cake and ask for four spoons to share, to the annoyance of the waitress. Andrei, who aspired to become a writer, read them his short stories and waited patiently for their 'crit'. Discussions became heated, each one of the group had a different view but after a few glasses of cheap wine they parted friends.

After a time, Myra began to miss her home and family and to look forward to their visits every month or two. Either Esther or Usher would arrive at her lodgings with bags full of goodies. In the evening Esther and Myra would go to the theatre or to the Light Opera House, and they discovered that they enjoyed each other's company.

On his visits, Usher would hire a carriage and they would take a ride along the Chaussee, a wide boulevard lined on each side with chestnut trees, leading to a triumphal arch and the newly-built Casa Scinteii, or House of the Press, built in the bombastic Stalinist style. Myra and her father visited cafeterias together, and the Circus, where they shared in the laughter at the antics of the clowns and marvelled at the skills of the trapeze artistes.

23
LETTERS TO FRIENDS

Dear Lilly,

Here I am, a student of medicine. I am living with a Mrs and Mr Perremisler, distant relatives of my mother. I so much wanted to go to the students' campus but they, meaning my delightful parents, would not let me, in case I should let my hair down.

Consequently I live in the entrance room of this ground floor flat, where light comes from above through a narrow, long window. When I look up I can see the pavement and if I am lucky legs moving to and fro. I don't always know whose legs I am seeing, my field of vision being limited. I can also see the side of the house, the entrance steps of the old service quarters, now inhabited by a family with many noisy children. One particular child seems to be causing a lot of trouble as he is restless and untamed.

My room is separated from my landlord's by a glass-panelled door and to go to the bathroom I have to pass through their room. It is not always convenient, but the flat is centrally situated and I have made friends with the caretaker. Her name is Madam Barbara. People say she is a police informer, but who isn't these days?

When I used to dream about being a med student, I thought it all would be lovely but, although I am very proud to be here I find it a little hard. All, or almost all, of my colleagues are older than me and they do not seem to pay any attention to me. The girls look so feminine and grown up with their pencil skirts and silk stockings and their hair cut in the most up to date styles. The boys vary: some are quite good looking. We also had an intake of students from the special school of the Party. They are much older and seem to come from factories or farms and had not received much schooling in their lives, but for the intensive special course. Every one of them has been put in charge of one of our study groups. Unfortunately Anca was placed in a group that has different timetables from mine so I am alone. Anca and I see each other almost every day and cannot stop chatting about our school and you and Christina.

Anca and I went to see Ony at the School of Architecture, which is not far from where I live. She seems to have settled in well. We found her in a long atelier, drawing the frontage of a building, with a radio set next to her playing light music. Her colleagues, bent over their working boards, seemed to be relaxed and cheerful. We came out thinking that those architects had a lovely time while we were stuck every day in the mortuaries, underground where the smell of formaldehyde made our eyes sore and our noses run. It is not fair.

Anca, as you know, is calm, but I am having a hard time. First of all I do not seem to retain anything I learn. I spend hours taking notes and revising and when the tutor asks me a question my mind goes blank. I freeze, I cannot utter a single sound. Everybody is looking at me, I can see they are thinking, 'how on earth did this one get in?' The tutor is quite venomous and sarcastic in his comments. He is an army doctor and behaves towards everyone like he probably addresses his soldiers.

I am almost desperate. I am lucky Anca is with me, reassuring and supporting me. She sends her love.

How are you? Is the course of advanced nursing interesting? How is Timishoara ? Have you made new friends? Write soon. I feel so lonely here. Myra

March 1955
Hi Lilly,

I was so happy to receive your letter and the photo. Anca and I barely recognised you: so grown up and attractive. Your hairstyle and everything is different, like you've entered a new world. Truly!

I am pleased you enjoy your studies and that you find enough time to go out dancing and clubbing. Have you met anybody nice?

Here, we are staying away from parties, trying to get to grips with anatomy and learn by heart all the bones and muscles and holes, their Latin names and their position in the human body. One day I brought home an arm and hand of a skeleton to revise. I was having breakfast and revising in the same time. My landlady happened to pass through my room on her way to the kitchen. The next thing I heard was her retching and being sick in the sink. I rushed to help her only to be greeted by her screaming at me to go away, accusing me of making her ill by eating my breakfast while touching those bones. I was perplexed and uncomprehending: why should the sight of bones make her ill.?

Apart from studying, I have made a few friends: Olga is a girl from Constantza and Lya, who is most impressive. She is a Greek with blond hair and blue eyes, very interested in fashion and style. She is two years older than me and looks like an ancient goddess. At lectures we sit together and at the labs we help each other. We are a little weary of some of our colleagues, particularly the communist one, designated to supervise us.

Most free time I spend at Anca's digs, in principle to revise for the exams but in reality to read detective novels and play with the house moggy, a beautiful Burmese cat with sharp claws. Anca seems to be totally uninterested in studies. She spends her time daydreaming, reading fiction, or going to the cinema. I spoke to Mrs Boiou about it when we went home for the winter break but she was not concerned, she said Anca worked hard for the entrance exam and she will start working again when she is ready. I was thinking of my parents who would give me such a hard time if they heard I was not working.

Anyway I seem to have overcome the fear or whatever it was and passed my exams with good marks. The tutor was quite surprised. He continues to have a negative attitude, especially towards the girls in the group, and also to have singled out Liviou, who is by far the cleverest and most knowledgeable of our group. He is the son of s doctor from Transylvania, a large chap with a face like a cherub. Dan Corbou is his best friend. He is also very tall, but thin and he walks with a stoop, making him look like a question mark. The two keep themselves to themselves. Anyway soon it will be the spring holidays and I hope we will meet. By the way, last Christmas I was invited to a party by a girl from the group next to ours, but Anca was not invited and I did not want to go by myself.

Hope to see you soon
Myra

Nov.1956
Dear Lilly.

I hope you are well. It is good to hear that you have passed the exam and that the retake was not so difficult.

Here, something dreadful has happened. I am not sure I should write this. In any case destroy this letter after reading it. Some of our colleagues, including Nicholas from our group have disappeared. There are rumours that they have been arrested. There is increased tension everywhere, the supervisors walk around with long faces and tight lips, and we have been informed that our study groups are to be dismantled and re-arranged. There is an undercurrent of fear and everybody seems to whisper rather than speak. Meetings with the leaders of the Youth Socialist Union are planned.

It appears that something like a rebellion happened in Hungary but the radio does not give much information. One of the boys who was arrested and kept overnight was released the next day. The others continue to be detained. He said that the day before his arrest, he got a phone call from Nicholas asking if they could meet in Victoria Place, near the University, and go to have a drink together. When he arrived, at around 8.0 in the evening, there were a few other boys there, chatting and waiting for their other mates to arrive. And all of a sudden they were surrounded by police and secret police in civilian clothes and arrested. He was interrogated all night, and released the next day. They wanted to know if he was part of the protest group, which he had never heard of. He does not know what happened to the others.

We had our meeting today, all our year was assembled. A chap from the central party committee attended. He talked very forcefully and made a lot of people stand up to be shown as propagators of capitalist symbols, among them, my friend Lya, who had just recently coloured her hair ash blonde. It was horrible. Our study group acquired a new girl – Aurore is her name – she talks a lot in a high soprano voice. Olga was moved away and some of the boys changed groups. We were warned, we are not allowed to meet privately. I wonder if it is the same at your school. I hope you keep away from all trouble. Please write if you can.

Love, Myra

Postcard

Dear Lily, Greetings from Constantza: our first holiday at the sea. I never dreamt it is so large and strong. We are staying with a relative of my friend Lya, very near the Casino. Lya and her cousin Spirou took me far into the sea to swim, I was frightened and elated all at the same time. It was marvelous. Mother and I got burned from the sun, but it was worth it. One good thing is that it stopped her wanting to take us to the mud baths of Tekirgoll at Eforie. I am reading Homer because he was exiled here in Tomis, as it was called. Hope to see you soon. Love M

24
A JOURNEY TO REMEMBER

The summer of 1957 Myra spent back home. She had to re-take one exam, the physiology exam had not gone very well. At the practical she had to experiment on a live frog and she had spent most of the allocated time trying to catch the slippery frog out of the sink. She could not complete the experiment and failed the exam. The plan to revise did not run smoothly. One night that summer her world turned upside down.

'What time is it? Myra woke up from a deep sleep. She rubbed her eyes and looked at the clock. Three o'clock in the morning. Why was the house ablaze with light?

'Mama, Daddy, what's going on?' No reply.

There were people in the house. She could hear them moving about.

'Mama, what is going on?' Again no answer.

Myra got up, put on her dressing gown on and went to the next room. She saw Dolly clinging to Mama, who was fully dressed and stood upright, silent, not moving, like a statue. The kitchen door was open and so was the front door. Not very far away muffled voices, men's voices, could be heard. Somebody was digging outside. Myra started walking towards the door, but Esther grabbed her and ordered her to stay where she was. Before Myra had time to protest three men stepped into the room: two strangers, with Usher between them. They walked past without even a glance at the mother and the girls, into the next room, and the next.

Esther turned to the girls. She whispered, 'You stay here!' and followed the men. Bea and Myra frose on the spot. They both knew something serious, beyond their understanding, had happened, something dreadful and threatening.

For a while, there was nothing. All was quiet.. Then the three men reappeared, Usher framed between the two strangers. Sudenly, he pulled away and he fell to his knees and started pleading with the men.

'Please, please, don't take me away. It was a mistake. Do you want money? I have money I will give you. My children...,' he continued, wailing.

Bea started crying and clung to him. Esther pulled her back. Myra remained standing, astounded at the scene taking place in front of her eyes. The only feeling she had,the only thought that passed through her mind was contempt for her father. How could a grown man, her father, get so low as to kneel in front of these men and cry like a helpless child? She felt ashamed for him and his loss of dignity.

The men did not even deign to notice Usher's distress. They pulled him up without a word, and dragged him out. A few more minutes and the sound of their vehicle started roaring then got quieter and quieter until it disappeared. Mother and children were left behind, with only Bea's whimpering in the silence.

Esther seemed to have lost the power of speech. Her steely eyes turned dull grey. Her hands were searching each other in despair. Then she started hitting the wall with her head. Her rhythmical movements increased the sense of panic and despair.

'Mama don't, please don't.' Myra and Bea clung to her trying to pull her away from the wall.

She stopped at last and looked at her two girls, her eyes traveling from the one to the other. What now? How will we be able to live again?

She seemed to recover her composure and she turned to Myra, determined and fully in control. 'You go,' she said.

'Where to, Mamma?'

'To Madam Segall. She always said if there is trouble she would help.'

'When, now? It's dark and she lives at the other end of town. Why do I have to go? Can't it wait till the morning? What is this all about anyway?'

'Questions, questions. Everybody asks me questions. Everybody wants answers from me. Those policemen. Your father. Now you.' And she started banging her head on the wall again.

After a while, she calmed down again. In a husky voice, almost a whisper, she started

'Look Myra, do you remember when Grandmother Anna came, before she left for Israel, to say goodbye to us? She brought a present for your Daddy, a legacy passed down through her family. As she was leaving for good, together with Aunt Clara and her husband, she made Daddy promise not to part with her gift in spite of the law passed by the government a few years ago by which it is forbidden to private citizens to own gold or any other precious goods.

154

All gold had to be given to the State. Your father, once he was told the story came home, without telling me, he dug a deep hole somewhere in the yard and buried his treasure that stayed there undisturbed for years, until this happened. Someone must have seen what he did, or he may have boasted to some of his friends. I don't know what to think.'

'So what will happen now?' asked Myra once she had found her voice. Lots of immages fought for attention in her brain. The pleasant life, the time away from home in Bucharest, carefree with her new friends, The holidays they had, the sea side, the mountains, all these will be gone for ever. She, most certainly will be sent home from the university; she most likely would have to get a job to support her mother and sister. And, what sort of job could she get? She was not trained to do anything; all her life till now was spent in learning, preparing herself for Medicine. She never thought before that Usher would not provide for the family.

'I don't know. I've heard that when someone is arrested the next day the police come and take everything from the house. I thought if you could take the money we keep in the house to Mrs Segall, at least we would have something to live on.' Esther said interrupting her thoughts

'No, Mamma. I'm scared. Isn't it better that you go?'

I can't. I can't! I can't leave you both alone in the house. What if I meet someone and they take me away as well?'

'What if someone stops me?'

'Nobody would suspect a young girl.'

'Where shall I put it? Is it a lot of money?'

'I have a money belt. We'll tie it round your middle. It won't show under the overcoat.'

'It's such a long way, and in the dark!'

'This is the only chance we have. This is the only way we can salvage something so we can go on! Please Myra!'

'All right. I'll go. Dolly, be good. Look after Mamma. Give me a cuddle,' Myra said to Bea and they fell into each other's arms.

The light was switched off. In almost total darkness the belt, bulging full of notes, was attached to Myra's body. Esther buttoned up Myra's coat and opened the door. The journey began.

The night loomed dark and menacing in its emptiness. The gate squeaked a little. In the distance a dog was barking and others joined in. Then all went quiet. Silence and blackness set like a heavy mantle on Myra's shoulders.

She turned her head and glimpsed the silhouettes of her mother and sister peering through the lace curtains. Farewell. I hope to be back, she thought.

Better not think at all, she decided. Just watch your step, Myra, she told herself.

Her shoes made a noise when they met the cobblestones of the road. It was not a loud noise but to Myra it sounded like thunder. The shoes were wrong. Better take them off. It was not easy to walk barefoot on uneven ground. She walked close to the houses hoping her small stature would not be noticed. The new moon did not give much light.

Another dog started howling from behind a locked gate. The surprise of it made Myra jump. She moved back to the middle of the road. At least the dogs would not wake up.

She made slow and painful progress. She stopped often on this uneven end of the High Street. The road was full of ruts. The stones were sharp and hurt her feet. The belt felt tight and stopped her breathing freely. She felt her pulse beating fast in her neck.

There was no wind. All was so quiet. The world was asleep, unaware of the drama. She alone was hurrying.

Myra reached the bend to the left in the road. On her right, in the deserted market the empty stalls stood like forlorn ghosts. She increased her pace in case some drunken men appeared from the darkness.

The High Street widened. The pavements were now even and smooth. Myra stopped and put her shoes on. From that point on, the street was lit by dim lights. She could see where she was going. She also knew she could be seen. She turned right at the first side street, as she decided it was safer to avoid the High Street and walk through the market, taking shelter behind the empty stalls.

She heard voices coming towards her. Just as well she turned the corner when she did. Now she flattened against the wall of the only large store in town, the Danube Magazine. Through a gap she saw two policemen walking along on patrol. She remained in place, her head down, until the sound of their boots faded in the distance.

She started walking again, tiptoeing around the market stalls, intent on any movement, any leaf that fell to the ground, any bird that flapped its wings, or the sound of anybody sleeping rough.

She reached the Station Road, which crossed the High Street. There were no trains at night and all was quiet. Myra stopped and checked to right and left for signs of night patrols. Her breathing was becoming shallow and her heart beat at a record rate. The thought of crossing the road in plain view, under the street lamps, took her strength away.

After a while she stood up and with determination hurried across the road, in her head already rehearsing what she would say if she was caught. She would say she was running away from home.

But that wouldn't be any good, she reasoned. The police would take her home and there the truth would come out. No. She would say she was a stranger and was lost. Perhaps they would believe that. Or she would say she had been sent for the doctor.

Nobody stopped her. A stray dog started to follow her. Myra became weary of it but the dog followed her quietly as if he needed a companion. There was no point in shooing him away. He might start barking.

On and on she walked until she reached the Independence Square. This was the biggest challenge. The Town Hall stood like a majestic shadow projected against the sky. This was the place where her picture once stood displayed on a stand as one of the best school achievers in town. That was long ago.

In the distance, on the opposite side of the square, the lighter outline of the Theatre Pastia looked ghostly white and the statue in the middle of the square all black. Behind the Town Hall stood the dreaded building of the Police Station. There was no way of avoiding it.

This was the crossing point from Moldavia into the Walachia side of the town. The place where the two ancient Principalities met. Here the road forked, Braila Street to the right. Memories flooded Myra's mind, making her forget for a short while of the danger she was in. She recalled the happy time when she lived with her grandparents in the grand villa, just before the war ended. The place her father came back to from the labour camp, looking like a beggar.

And look where she was now. On the run again. Not of her own doing.

Resigned, she walked on. Nobody interrupted her walk along Braila Street, past the large villas surrounded by the large gardens with iron railings pointing sharp to the sky.

Not far now. Soon, Myra hoped, she would be relieved of the menacing burden sitting hot on her body. As she neared her destination she began to have doubts. What if nobody answered her call? What if the Segalls did not want the responsibility and turned her away? It would be daylight by then and she would be spotted going back.

There would be questions. What was she doing on the street out at that early hour?

She knocked. Mr Segall came to the gate. He did not ask. He just took her quickly indoors. Mrs Segall appeared in her dressing gown thrown over her pajamas. The couple understood immediately. It was as if everybody in town was prepared for such events, and ready to help each other in case of trouble.

Without a word Mrs Segal took the belt off Myra's chest and laid the table for breakfast.

Myra came back home in broad daylight. She felt exhausted and numb, her mind racing. Why, why, she asked herself. She found her mother and sister huddled together in the front room where she had left them, in semi-darkness, the curtains drawn. They were relieved to see her. Myra was back, she was safe and they fell into each other's arms in a tight embrace. They stayed close for a while, each one with her own thoughts. Myra was trying to picture where her father was. Was he in a cell? Had he been beaten up? What was going to happen next?

Nobody came to the house. As darkness fell again, Esther stirred. She had to do something. She knew from what others had endured, that an arrest would be followed by a police raid and they were at liberty to seize all their worldly goods. She knew she had to save what she could.

She went to the neighbours. They already knew and understood, and they offered to take some of Usher's clothes. He had been a smart dresser. When he could afford it, he bought good quality fabrics from people who had parcels sent to them by relatives who lived in the West. He had good suits made to measure, good shoes, a good, fur lined winter coat.

Marianna, Esther's school friend who lived across the road, offered to help save Esther's and the children's clothes. She knew that the policemen would help themselves to anything they fancied before a trial or a sentence was passed. So the second evening was spent filling suitcases and baskets with the family possessions and carrying them in the dark to the homes of willing neighbours.

Finally they had something to eat and settled down for the night, but sleep would not come.

'Why, mama? Why has all this had to happen?'

It took Esther a long time to start talking, haltingly, trying to find the right words to explain.

'You may have noticed that your father has started to come home late, the last few nights. That was because he was summoned to the police station for an interview. They questioned him about the possession of gold coins. He denied everything. The next evening he was called in again and interrogated. This time, from the next room, came the sound of women voices screaming as if they were tortured and in pain. The policemen who were interrogating told him, 'Look what we do to women if their men don't come clean. We get the truth out of them and out of you.' Every night he came home so scared, we did not get much sleep.'

'So why didn't he declare it, from the beginning when the law was passed?' asked the girls.

'Remember Bunica Anna's last visit.? She brought with her a few gold French coins which had been in her family for generations, to be handed on to the next generation. She entrusted her little fortune to your father for safekeeping. He did not want to part with his inheritance, he wanted to make sure you, his daughters would inherit, it would be for your future, he said. He had kept the gold. He dug a hole in the garden and the seventy gold coins stayed buried there.

'That is, until the last few months. One of his so-called friends introduced him to someone who was dealing in gold on the black market. No matter how much I tried to talk him out of it he was determined to buy some more. He said it was safe.

'So look how safe it was. That 'friend' or his contact was obviously an informer, and Usher fell into the trap. Now what are we going to do?'

'Madam Segal said we should get a solicitor.'

'Yes, perhaps. I think that will be another job for you, Myra, you can speak more convincingly than me, I do not know of any solicitor and I don't think it would help, Anyway I just cannot face all this. The shame!' Esther sounded defeated.

'What are you talking about, Mother, we cannot abandon him there. I am going to try and find out where he is and if there is going to be a trial.'

'Oh, I don't know, I expect we'll hear soon enough. What will be, will be'

Myra vaguely remembered her physics teacher, Mrs Ciuley, and her husband. He had lost a leg in the war. She remembered that he was a solicitor. He would put her on the right track. She discussed it with Esther and they agreed that she should call on him.

The next day Myra set off for the Ciuleys' home. She reached the wrought iron gates in the road to the Theatre Pastia. The elegant villa, once white, seemed deserted. She knocked and knocked. After a while she heard shuffling footsteps. Mr Ciuley opened the door, looking barely recognisable, haggard and much older.

No, he said, he could not take the case. He was no longer in practice. Even if he was still working he wouldn't take the case as it would be a waste of his time and their money. In such cases the outcome was already decided, even before coming to court. The trial was a formality, the defence just for show.

'Surely we can do something,' said Myra.

Perhaps, he said, if she went to the county town at Galatzi she might find someone willing to swear the coins were inherited and perhaps get a reduced sentence.

Deeply disappointed, Myra returned home. Esther did not know what to do. She kept wringing her hands in despair. Myra said she would go to Galatzi by train, to find out when the trial was to be held and to enquire after a solicitor. Esther agreed.

The police showed up without delay, as expected. They came with a van and emptied the house. They left one suit in the wardrobe, along with Esther's and the family's remaining clothes, which had been left so as not to draw attention to an empty cupboard. They took everything of any value, including the piano, the easy chairs and the tables. They left behind two beds, one cupboard, one table and four chairs. At least they did not touch the kitchen.

When Esther insisted on knowing where her husband was, one of the men told her that Usher was still in the local jail and would be transferred to Galatzi in three weeks' time to stand trial.

Myra started making inquiries about train timetables and where to stay overnight, and a few days later she boarded the train to Galatzi. An imposing town on the banks of the Danube, the county town showed signs of past solidity and prosperity as the once important harbour that was. There were solid buildings, wide streets, statues and fountains, testimonies of a better time.

All Myra's hopes vanished at the Law Courts. A solicitor for the defence had already been appointed by the court. Myra asked to see him. He agreed to meet her, only to tell her the trial was a formality and the sentence was already prescribed by law. For the 70 gold coins Usher would be sent to prison for seven years. There was no point hanging about. She went back to the station and took the late evening train home.

So life began a new phase. Without her father Mayra had to go back to university, leaving a distraught mother and a frightened sister behind. The holiday was over. She wondered how long it would be before the news of her father's arrest reached the med school authorities and what would happen then. She was hoping it would be after the trial, or perhaps never.

When she recovered from the shock and started to organise her thoughts, Esther went to see some people she knew in the organisation where Usher worked and applied for a job. She started work as an administrator's clerk and after a while she was found capable and diligent and rose to the position of Administrator. It was in that roundabout way that Esther's early vow to be an independent woman finally was fulfilled.

Usher was duly sentenced to seven years in prison.

Back at Medical school Myra confided only in Anca, her best friend and her support during the time of great anxiety and insecurity. She waited day after day for the dreadful letter that would inform her she could no longer pursue her studies. It went on and on for almost one year and then, the monthly grant of three hundred lei stopped abruptly. Her landlady agreed to forgo the rent till Myra had a chance to speak to Esther. But Esther insisted that the money saved at the Segalls' during that nightmarish night was to be kept for Bea and herself and for parcels for Usher.

Myra's hopes appeared shattered. Anca offered that they should move in together, but Myra was uneasy, she was unwilling to accept. She needed a long term plan.

When the summons came from the college authorities Myra knew she would soon have to appear before the UTM (Union of Youth Workers) leaders and she tried to prepare a good story. Nothing happened, and she did not dare inquire about her grant. Life became increasingly hard. She borrowed money from Anca and persuaded Esther at least to pay the rent for the room.

One day the letter came summoning her to the dreaded interview. With shaking hands Myra opened the envelope which bore the university logo. It sounded like bad news. Perhaps the decision had already been taken. Perhaps she was going to be thrown out, after all her hard work. What would she do? The call was from the Deanery.

On the day of the interview Myra tied her hair up in a bun, dressed in a skirt and a top buttoned up to the neck in order to avoid any suggestion of frivolity. Her stomach was churning and she was afraid she would loose control of her bladder, or break down in front of all those people. The secretary greeted her and asked her to wait. After what seemed ages she was asked in and closed the door behind her.

The Dean of the university sat, looking larger than life, on a leather chair behind a large ornate desk. A pale ray of sunshine found a way between the drawn curtains and fell on his hands. He was alone, and he asked the secretary to leave the room. The sun was shining a cold white light through the large window, making every object glimmer like ice.

Myra was invited to sit. The large chair almost engulfed her, although she sat on the very edge of the seat.

The Dean, a well-known professor and famous surgeon who was known for his direct approach, came straight to the case in hand.

He said, 'I asked you to come here alone, before other people became aware of your unfortunate circumstances, to advise you that the only way you can continue your studies is to take a job, become independent and disengage from any contact with the criminal activities of your family.'

Myra was stunned, struck dumb. After a while she managed to say, 'Thank you.' She gave way to floods of tears.

The Dean stood up and said, 'You may go now. This conversation never took place.'

Myra stood up and made her way out. The secretary busied herself at her desk, never lifting her eyes from her work.

Myra was in a trance. She felt sick. She ran to the nearest toilet and vomited. She washed her face, cleaned herself and came out smiling.

She could stay! She had to find a job. There was hope after all!

PART 2

25
MARRIAGE

Myra and Dan married in August 1961.It was a simple ceremony at the Registry Office, followed by a lovely meal given in the bride and groom's honour by Nelly, one of Myra's closest friends. Nelly's brother, the only one who had a photo camera, was appointed the wedding photographer. It was a happy occasion. It would have been happier if some of the most important people in Myra's life had been present. For Esther and Bea were not there. She did not want to think about that, she would deal with it later. She must concentrate and enjoy her day.

She wore her new dress made by Olivia's mother, another one of her friends. It was not a wedding dress, like in the fairy tales of long ago. Nobody wore those anymore, just a nice white summer dress. Her girlfriends were her bridesmaids, Lya, Dora, Aurora. There were lots of guests: Usher, her father, recently released from prison looking older but happy, two of Usher's cousins, Montzy and Victor and all Dan's family: his parents, his aunts and their husbands, friends of Dan and his family and Myra's friends. All but Anca, who from the start had resented Myra's friendship with Dan. Much, much later Myra would discover that Anca's feelings went beyond a schoolgirl's friendship and often she would feel sorry for Anca and guilty for never having   understood.

They ate and drank and took pictures. It was a lovely day full of hope and laughter.

Myra did not want to think that Esther had let her down once again but the thoughts broke through, no matter how hard she tried to brush them away.

Myra swept the nagging thoughts out of her head. A new life was in front of her, the prospect of perhaps a better placement as a doctor nearer home with the support of a loving husband. She was in love with Dan; she loved and embraced his family who offered her warmth and respect. She was a Doctor and soon would be a married woman. However she had not recovered from the surprise: two months ago Esther and Usher had agreed to the marriage. What a troubled day that had been.

It was a Sunday morning, the rain had fallen all night but the sun was already shining on the wet surface of the leaves and pavements. What a lovely day for a walk in the park, Myra thought. She will call Dan and suggest they go for a picnic. She had had enough time over night to think over Dan proposal.

He had said in a quiet, almost understated way -that it was better for them both to be together and to have a place of work as near as possible to home in Bucharest. He could not follow her, as that would mean losing his job and the right to live and work in the capital. And, once that right was lost it would be very difficult to regain the authorisation to come back. They would live for a while with his parents while she had to fulfil her duty and work where the authorities would send her, in a village away from home. After serving the compulsury three years, she could return to Bucharest and they would make plans to leave the country, perhaps persuade Myra's parents to apply for emigration to Israel. Myra and Dan could apply together with them. He seemed to have it all worked out. His big dream was to leave the country and return to England where he spent his early childhood. But Myra, who had avoided thinking about it previously, needed time to ponder. She dreaded her parents' reaction at this mixed faith marriage and could not see herself facing them. She had to admit to herself that Dan and she were an item, that they loved each other and they were above all very good friends. The fact that they were brought up in different religions, she a Jewish girl and he as a Christian did not worry either of them but this may cause a problem with their respective families. At the same time she had to face the fact that separation at this late stage in their relationship was going to be very painful. Hence, she found it easier not to think about it at all.

But, Dan had different ideas. He wanted to get married and could not understand Myra's reluctance to approach the subject with her parents. He believed in real facts: they were in love they made a good couple; religion, beliefs, all those belonged to another time, a time long overtaken by the present.

Dan was determined to do things properly and went to ask Myra's parents for her hand in marriage. And so that Sunday morning in May, Myra found out that Dan accompanied by his father had left early and travelled to Focsani. Myra felt the ground disappearing from under her feet. She was sure her parents would not even receive them. What embarrassment! She was angry. How could he take such liberties when she had not given him a definite answer? At the same time a surge of hope rose amongst the wrath and fear, and a tiny glimpse into a brighter future appeared on the horizon. Marriage, career, perhaps children, all those prospects were standing in front of her and she could in time reach them if all went well. But then the fear returned: what if they refused? What would she do? She would have to make a decision. If they were rude to Dan and his father? The friendship with him and his whole family where she felt at home and wished to be part of her life would have to cease. She would have to undo all that happened during those last important years of her life.

Myra's thoughts drifted back to the beginning. How surprised she had been and she had wondered how come the family, who lived in the apartment on the first floor, had found out she was a medical student. She had never met them. The logical explanation was that it came from Madame Barbara, the caretaker and resident gossip. She was the one poking her nose in everyone else's business; everyone suspected that she was an informer for the Securitate.

That time though, it had suited Myra well and she had welcomed the request from the neighbours for some paid work since she was broke .

The part time nurse job she was able to find after losing her grant, paid very little. Myra worked every afternoon while in the morning she attended courses, wrote her dissertation, and worked in the hospital wards.

The man who knocked at her door that evening looked innocent enough. Middle aged, clean shaven, the only think that had startled her was his moustache, Hitler style. The resemblance was enhanced by his dark complexion and piercing eyes under hooded eyelids and his gaunt, lined face. However his smile was reassuring. He enquired politely about the possibility of her giving penicillin by injections to his son, who had been injured at work. Myra thought how little attention she had given to her neighbourhood; she had never met these neighbours, although the man said they had been living in the same building for the last three years.

She said she was going to think over the offer and would reply soon.

Immediately after he left, Myra ran downstairs and knocked at Madame Barbara's door. She was the eyes and ears of Udrican 24.

Within minutes Myra found out all she wanted to know. The family in question had moved in, as the man had said, three years previously. Husband, wife and three children; two were grown up. They either went to work or they were students. Barbara said she watched them leaving early at the same time each morning. There was a much younger girl who was attending the local school.

'Perhaps they don't belong to the same father,' Barbara said, winking suggestively. Myra smiled politely.

'The wife has a job as well, only the man does not seem to go to work, but I have noticed, only by accident mind you, when I was cleaning the back staircase, he is doing the cooking and the shopping. You can see him coming in the morning with his net shopping bag in one hand and his newspaper tucked under his arm.'

Myra listened, saying nothing. Madame Barbara carried on wondering out loud where they came from and what were they living on if the man did not have a paid job. She was hoping once Myra went into their home, she would find out a little more about that odd family and would be willing to share the information.

Myra left as soon as she could and knocked at the family's door. There was no reply and she pushed a little note through the door saying she was going to take the job.

On the first day Myra was a little anxious. It was her first private job. .She dressed up for the occasion and after some deep breathing exercises to calm her nerves, she went to meet her patient. Guided by Dan's father she entered the small bedroom, fighting her way past the family dog. Greetings and introductions were exchanged. The young man, in his twenties, or perhaps a little older, occupied the bed in the small room, which was reached after passing through several other rooms. He greeted Myra with an apologetic smile in his immobile state, the plaster cast on his foot visible under the blanket. She had a struggle to give him the injection as the dog was determined to come between Myra and his master.

She did not look at him directly, busying herself with setting up syringes, swabs, needles, checking the batch and date on the penicillin bottle, looking most professional. So, in effect, the first part she ever saw of Dan was his slim bottom.. The conversation was mostly about the dog's name. He was called Sesar, a name chosen by Amy, the younger sister. It was the family name in reverse Myra was told. He was a young gun dog, unruly and up to mischief. Myra went afterwards to the bathroom to clean the instruments but she took one look at the grime covered sink and changed her mind. She would do that at home. Her first impression consolidated in the following few days. They were a once-upon-a time well to do, educated family, a little unfamiliar with normal domestic jobs, stuck together, and living in impoverished circumstances. That was not unusual in the late fifties.

Myra was given a key and asked to come anytime and to let herself in, once she familiarised herself with the place. The second or the third day she let herself into the apartment and noticed that no other member of the family was present. That made her nervous. But she gave her patient the injection and inquired about his progress. He had a pleasant baritone voice and a friendly smile. He played down his discomfort, peppering his words with a few jokes, which made Myra smile. She became more relaxed and at ease. .

During her daily visits she had met most of the people living in the apartment. They were George, the elder man she had already met, Silky his wife, a peroxide blonde of a certain age, Dan the young man with his plastered injured foot, her patient. And Sesar who jumped on her chest and with whom the battle became a daily routine. There was Lydia, only a couple of years younger than her brother, both in their mid-twenties and the youngest, Amy a lively eleven years old. Myra became familiar with their apartment, with its atmosphere of almost mysterious decay. The entrance hall housed an old-fashioned coat stand, which occupied almost the whole space, full of coats of different sizes. A fur coat most likely in fashion before the war, lay next to good quality well-worn men's coats, above which there were men's grey and black hats such as one saw those days only in American movies. The hall opened into a large room full of antique furniture , worn out, the wood chipped but still elegant in that decaying sort of way. A large desk covered in tattered leather full of papers and newspapers and a typewriter ready for work. Against the wall, near the entrance was a single bed. A high arcade separated this room from the second room giving the feeling of a much larger space. This was enhanced by a large mirror which occupied almost the entire wall opposite the window, reflecting and amplifying the light. The dining room furniture, light walnut wood and beautiful high back chairs, transported the visitor into the jazz times of the thirties, the feeling only disturbed by the presence of yet another bed tucked in a corner. The dining room opened through glass panelled doors into another room, a proper bedroom with dark oak furniture and lamps hidden behind shades. At the far end a door led to a bathroom and on the other side to a tiny room, where the the object of her visit lay. There was a faint hint, of moth balls in the air. Myra's imagination took flight. She could see in her mind this elegant apartment once belonging to a young couple, a mother, father and a young child in the nursery room with the elegant dining room for entertaining and the reception room. A servant in a black dress with a white starched apron would greet her at the door. All that was gone now and the apartment was accommodating a much larger family who made do with little space for themselves. Still they were luckier then most, not having to share with strangers. So many other families had to live with total strangers ,sharing kitchens and bathrooms lacking privacy. Eight cubic meters of living space was the allowance per individual, privacy was not considered essential.

The last day of treatment arrived. Her patient was again alone in the house. Once her duties had been completed, Myra wished him all the best and started to say goodbye when Dan came forward limping, shook her hand and gave her a kiss. 'Thank you for all you've done,' he said. Myra felt the blood rising in her cheeks and turned and left abruptly. But Myra could not get the event out of her mind. Two weeks later she received a thank you card and an invitation to go and see a film together when he was be able to walk again. Myra did not reply or take up the invitation, too busy with studies and work. Besides, her fear of getting tangled in a close relationship with a young man she reluctantly admitted to herself that she liked, but who belonged to a different world, prevented her to getting closer.

The opportunity to meet again arose just before Christmas 1959. Myra received a letter inviting her to a Christmas Eve party. Her patient was by then fully recovered, she presumed he was back at work. She had learned he was employed as an assistant engineer at a large factory specialising in building tractors while continuing his university studies at night school.. She was pleased to accept the invitation. At that time she could not afford the fares home to Focsani and she was facing the prospect of spending Christmas alone. Anca had gone home for Christmas and so had all her other friends   .

On Christmas Eve she put her best clothes on and waited till she could hear voices and steps climbing to the first floor. She did not want to be the first to arrive. She climbed the few steps and rang the doorbell. Laughter and songs seeped out. George opened the door. He was wearing a lounge suit, He was tired looking, his coat was crumpled and a dark tie was askew round his neck. His shiny black eyes creased in a smile. He looked even older than last time Myra had met him, his receding hair line even further back than before, the few strands of black hair that were left, skilfully arranged on top of his head. The sitting room and the dining room were decorated with garlands of red and yellow crimped paper. The young man who for two weeks had endured Myra's ministrations was sitting on a chair surrounded by people she did not know. He wore dark round glasses and a pipe was smoking peacefully in the corner of his delicately shaped mouth, making him quite attractive in a Hollywood sort of way. He was even more attractive in the flesh than when Myra was thinking of him. He introduced Myra to his friends. Lydia his sister was there with some of her university colleagues. She studied electronics at the Polytechnic School. She looked pretty but her face was sad and angry. Myra was to find out later from her mother that she was sulking because her father George did not accept her boyfriend and had banned him from attending the family gathering. It appeared her friend's political leaning towards communism put him in conflict with the views of the head of the family.

There were people of all ages at the party; among whom a middle aged couple stood out. The gaunt man, who was chain smoking, was George's youngest brother, Constantin. He used an expletive every time he opened his mouth- to

179

the discomfiture of everybody else. Some people use swear words to be expressive and emphatic, but when an expletive entered this man's mouth the word filled his mouth and he spat out with full force. Most of his venom was addressed to the political powers and the law. George was trying without success to calm him down and Silky was almost in tears .The others were either laughing, embarrassed, or trying to ignore him. Myra felt very uncomfortable.

'Don't take any notice of Costantin, I'd rather we spend some time getting to know each other a little better,' Dan said.

Myra sat down by his side, suddenly feeling shy. What was there to say about herself? That she was Jewish? It was a Christmas party and she felt that this would make a bad impression. She could not talk about her father who was still away. She could not say that she does not have a boyfriend without feeling that she is becoming too forward and intimate.

Seeing that Myra was quiet, Dan started the conversation.

He told her how the family was split during the war years, how he, Lydia and their mother spent most of those years in London while his father was with the Allied Forces in the Middle East, how he went to school in London at a girl's school in Kensington, the boy's school having suffered from the bombardment and been closed. When they returned to Romania in '46, neither he nor Lydia spoke Romanian and had to learn the language again. The room became quiet, everybody listening; proof that the goal was achieved. It was a good opportunity for George to take up the story, to explain how he was a journalist who rose against fascism, which was spreading into the country before the war and had been hunted by the fascists in Romania. He was forced to flee the country and find refuge for himself and his family in Turkey where he was recruited and joined the Special Forces and together with other journalists formed a group with a radio station from which they transmitted, asking the people of Romania to denounce the alliance with Germany and turn their arms against the Nazis. The group headquarters moved from Istanbul to Jerusalem and as Rommel's offensive advanced into North Africa, they moved to Cairo where the work on the radio continued.

The danger was near and the British Command decided to move the women and children of all the active personnel in the Allied Forces to London for safety. Silky and the two children were shipped abroad on the Queen Mary. They took the long route round the Cape to England, the Suez Canal being closed. They lived in London on half of George's monthly pay. When the war was over George was demobilised and he opted to return to the country he fought so hard to liberate. He persuaded his wife and children to return and start anew. In 1946 they boarded a ship in Liverpool and made the journey back. As the Iron Curtain fell across Europe old allies became enemies and George was arrested and imprisoned by the Soviets who occupied Romania. Overnight he changed from a hero into a British spy. He spent five years in prison and had come out three years before, physically weak, prematurely aged and morally almost destroyed.

Well, what a story! Myra's head was buzzing with conflicting thoughts. This was Christmas 1958 and she felt she should not be there, that it was dangerous to mix with such people. At the same time she felt admiration, respect and a great deal of sorrow for this family. The quiet was broken by George's brother who loudly said. 'And now what do you want? A medal for being an idiot and coming back here?' Everybody felt it was time for some music and dance. Dan excused himself for not dancing and Myra spent a lot of time in his company that evening. She was fascinated by the story Dan had told her. She felt at ease in his company.

She listened to Dan's father's stories of the war, which had been, it appeared, for them, the most important time in their lives and shaped theirs and their children's future.

A few days later Myra received a note from Dan. Inviting her again to see a film .This time she said 'yes'.

They met in the yard outside the building. It was a dull winter day and she wore her winter coat. He had a long grey overcoat and a grey hat. He carried a walking stick in his right hand as he was still walking with a limp.

His smile was wide and he looked handsome, albeit old fashioned and very thin. The film they went to see was 'Les Enfants du Paradise' with Gerard Phillipe, whom, indeed, Dan resembled a little (as he had previously pointed out). They held hands during the film and left politely thanking each other for the company.

The winter dark engulfed the street, the mantle of cold weather descended but Myra was not touched by it. She had new friends and she went to have tea with them, eager to listen to more stories. Those people were so different from her own family, from the way Myra was brought up. Their house was always open to their children's friends. They were poor but there was always a cup of tea and a biscuit for any visitor. Myra could imagine Esther's stern face, her pursed lips when any one called on her or her sister, Usher's inquisitorial enquiries if Myra was late or Anna, her landlady's reported that she had gone out with friends Besides, that family had the secret of their past, their determination to survive and leave the country. Myra had her secret too; her father was in prison for possessing something that belonged to him in the first place, but he did not comply with the draconian law. And in spite of her instincts, Myra could not resist the attraction of her new friends, especially Dan and became a regular visitor at the apartment on the first floor. Friendship blossomed. She was gradually falling in love with Dan, and he with her. They discovered that they had a lot in common, their views, their beliefs. They started to see each other as often as they could. Every night, when Myra returned from her nursing job and

Dan from the factory, they met briefly for a little company, talk about their day and tired they parted with a kiss.

They both had to prepare for the final exams and their graduation projects. Dan's project had to be hand-drawn, all the graphs and designs precise, and labelled by hand in clear calligraphy. He was too tired in the evenings to trust his hand so he enlisted the help of his father, who had beautiful handwriting. Being unemployed, George was glad to help.

Myra had to apply herself to finish her research project into Hypertension and unilateral kidney disease and for this she had to find time during the day and go to the medical library and read articles related to her subject. This was almost impossible with her time commitments, so, once again George volunteered to go instead, read and summarise the information. He was pleased to be useful and be the journalist again and Myra was grateful.

Slowly Myra and Dan started to spend the evenings together in the first floor apartment. They sat till late into the night, on opposite sides of George's large desk, writing and reading and dozing off from time to time when fatigue got the better of them. They felt happy and found strength in each other. Myra refused to acknowledge that this was more than a close friendship and would not lead to any good in her already troubled circumstances. She felt that when the two of them had met there was nothing to suggest romance. It was an accident of fate that developed further than they thought. And when the time was be right, they would part in the best of terms Her landlady and her friend Anca warned her not to get too close but she felt involved. She had to know more, know him better. Besides, the atmosphere in the flat upstairs, somehow felt like home.

26
GEORGE AND SILKY

George had not been able to find work after he was released from prison. He was frail and demoralised. All the friends in high places he had had before appeared to avoid him. He spent most of his time brooding. Silky, who managed to find a job as a primary school teacher, would come home from work tired and quarrelsome. She expected George to take charge of all domestic chores. Myra could hear them from the kitchen of her flat arguing with raised voices. Who could blame Silky, she thought. She was complaining that the headmistress at the school where she was working treated her like a second-class citizen. The woman was a devout Party member. The family were short of money and Silky felt George was not pulling his weight. She often came down to Myra's flat to unburden herself. She resented the fact that once he was back home, he had reinstated his total authority as the head of the family.

Silky shuddered remembering those years, the daily walk to the village school where she was exiled to, which was on the outskirts of the town. There was no direct access, the bus from RATA always late, always crowded, and would leave her a mile from the school in the middle of the empty road. Myra felt for her, thinking of the life she could have had if she had remained in England. However Silky loved her man; he was her hero. She fought as hard as she could to get him out of prison and see him home. During the five long years he was away, unable to contact him or to find out if he was alive or dead she had knocked repeatedly at all the important doors, had queued for audience with all the important men and women they had known before they had fallen from grace. She had worked all the overtime she could get to insure the children did no go hungry. When Lydia was admitted to the University she was proud and happy. Myra understood how Silky must have felt when she told her how her son, who dreamt of becoming a theatre producer, had applied to art drama school as soon he had passed his baccalaureate. His application was rejected on account of what was considered by the authorities that he was unsuitable, with a dangerous, undesirable background. She was upset for him, however in a way, she was glad he did not go into the arts. He had found a job as an apprentice driver for a building firm and put his name down for a course in engineering at the night school. She remembered, looking at his face, how tired he was when he came from work, barely keeping his eyes open and starting to work for his course. Still, there was a little more money coming in and with a bit of luck he would graduate and have a solid, down to earth profession. Not like his father…Silky said with a hint of bitterness in her voice. George had come back in 1955 and once back, the old problems surfaced again. His habit of paying attention to younger women, even his friends' wives made her angry and jealous.

George was thinking. He found he had a lot of time to think, to find the place of his life in the grand scheme of things. Every morning Silky left him a list of jobs for the day and the money for the food he was supposed to try and find in the various empty shops.This came with a stern warning: 'You have plenty of time to queue and please do not spend money on newspapers or flowers for your beloved friend Ileana,' she would say and her bright blue eyes would turn green.

'Silky is still pretty,' he thought watching her, even if the years and hardship had carved deep lines on her baby face. He loved her. If only she would not make such a show of being the breadwinner. If only she knew how much it hurts. Myra often found him curled up in bed during the day. It was quiet, the house still bearing the print of the family who left to work. He was the only one who could not find work. He would rather stay in bed and think of the book he would start writing soon, perhaps when the pain of the interrogations and humiliations he had suffered in prison had eased.

The problem was that Silky was going on and on about it. It was her greatest ambition- to see her hero, the husband she had sacrificed so much for, become again the revered journalist, the man who played such an important role during the war.'She does not have any deep insight, all is black and white in her simple mind,' he told Myra one time. 'She thinks her hard work and earning money requires an immediate return.' There was no pity in her for his disappointment and sufferings. 'She does not understand that a writer needs time to think and research documents and papers and this is not possible with the permanent malevolent surveillance of the Securitate. She does not understand me.'

He would get up and get dressed and go to Ileana's... He would spend the rest of the day reading his papers at Ileana's, his friend for as long as he could remember; perhaps he would help her son with his homework. She would comfort and understand. Besides, she made lovely coffee.

'Look at the time! Soon they will all be back from work and I have not done the shopping or anything. Good Lord, what will Silky say?' George started to panic. Ileana hastily packed a few tins, some vegetables and bread from her supply. Her husband, a well-connected engineer, brought home more food items from the special shops than the family could consume. Laden with these goods, George would get home as fast as he could and prepare something for the hungry lot. Two grown up children and a school girl required plenty of nourishment.

Silky arrived home as usual at 5 o'clock .She was still smarting from the sermon this new Headmistress, gave her for being late. It was simply persecution by this Communist

She tried to talk, to unburden herself, but the house is empty. She knew where George might be. She went to the kitchen, opened the back door and called Myra. Myra was a good listener. After a while, Silky invariably turned the conversation back to the war. She talked of the war as the best years of her life, spent abroad. Nobody from her family had ever set foot outside the country before that. She remembered the nights spent in Istanbul in Pera, the expensive European area. She talked of the time spent in Palestine with her man and her two young children, he the journalist broadcasting to Romania. She was so proud of him, proud herself then, she was young and the life at King David hotel in Jerusalem was like a dream. This made her forgive her philandering husband's on- and-off escapades. He always returned to her and the children. The worst was when he insisted that he was right and she was wrong, that she had just imagined what was obvious. It was always her fault and in the end, for the sake of peace she would say that she was convinced and it was she who had to apologise to him. 'Oh,' she said with a sigh, dreaming of those good old days, when among the group of dissidents gathered at the Romanian Church in Jerusalem she was the most beautiful of all the wives. Her son, only seven years old, sitting with the men and talking of the important issues with a maturity beyond his years. It made her so proud. She could not forget, nor could she give in. 'He must start writing!' 'Then we moved to Cairo with the new location of the allied quarters. We had a lovely apartment in Gezira. The children went to the English School, we had servants and we were invited to all high Egyptian Society parties.'

Her face suddenly darkened and her eyes turned grey. 'Then, what did my silly husband do? He had a new affair, this time with an Egyptian socialite. The wife of a General, no less.'

When the time came, she did not regret the evacuation of women and children to London; it was considered dangerous for them to stay on. On the contrary she welcomed it. George's last affair was just too much. From far away, George wrote very loving letters to his children. For them, mostly for Dan, their father was their hero. Lydia only worried that the Germans took away bananas from the children and she loved bananas. Silky smiled among tears. The three of them lived through bombardments and v-bombs closer than ever but, she missed George and the children missed their father. Her only regret now, was to have believed in him when he had written at the end of the war, that he had changed, that he loved her and missed her and he had persuaded her to return to their liberated, free country. She left London behind and in ' 46, she and the children boarded a ship from Liverpool. The reunion went well. For the first two years all doors opened to them, the couple who had come back from exile and contributed to free their country. She never asked what happened to the beautiful Assrar, the General's wife; she guessed she must have gone back to her husband. 'All the more fool him,' she said, grinning. When she discovered that she was pregnant, she was beside herself, she did not want another child, not then. Those were not times to have children. Besides, the elder children needed all her help to re-adjust to their new life. What about the English-speaking nursery she had started, what about the piece of land they bought where they had plans to build a house of their own? But George was totally opposed to her having an abortion and as usual he won. She gave birth to a girl, but may God forgive her she said, she never took to her. 'Look, look Myra,' she said. 'He is not here, there is nothing done, no provisions, no food on the stove. He probably is having a jolly good time at Ileana's. To think how I struggle to keep this family together and he is not doing anything to help me, he only does what suits him. Promises he will write but he is not really writing either.'

At other times Silky remembered the harsh winters when she had to walk on foot through snow drifts to the village school where she was sent to teach like an exile after George's arrest; the arduous journeys she took to petition all the old friends still in power who gave her the cold shoulder and ignored her pleas. It took her five years of her life to set him free and a long time to make him to regain his health. The search for employment for George proved fruitless, he was too frail for the low paid physical work that was offered to him He remained undesirable, an enemy of the state and all requests for better jobs were dismissed or ignored. So life continued day after day George and Silky would quarrel in the morning, then silence would prevail most of the day and in the evening, seeing them hand in hand Myra was sure they were off to see Ileana. Myra felt sorry for her, for all her yearnings and unfulfilled dreams ly bring misfortune and further persecution for her.

In spite of the growing attraction for Dan, Myra still had doubts. She thought once she graduated, they would be separated and that distance would diminish the feelings they had for each other. Then she remembered how much she was looking forward to coming home, tired from her afternoon shift, to a warm reception in the family who always found an extra bowl of beans soup or plum dumplings, dishes that Silky cooked from their meagre income, to offer. Myra found herself trust in a position of a councillor and a friend to the older woman although she did not feel that she was qualified for that job. She was too young for that.

Visits to Anca became less frequent, as she appeared not to enjoy Myra's stories and refused to join in with the new group of friends. Anca became less and less occupied with her studies; she was daydreaming of distant shores Myra could not reach. Imperceptibly the string that joined the two friends together became thinner than a spider's thread. It was time to move on. Meantime Lya was in love. She met a suave man with a beard and delicate manners, a descendent of the old aristocracy, in his forties with no evidence of regular employment. He taught her all there was to know about love and she was besotted with him. Her parents were besides themselves with worry and appealed to Myra to try and dissuade Lya from continuing with that relationship. As expected that only led to a cooling of the friendship between the two girls, but in time they made up.

The last exams took place in May and Myra passed with very good grades. Dan graduated from the Institute of engineering and had his diploma. Myra and Lya had one more assignment before presenting their Doctorate project, six weeks' attachment to a general practice. They chose the town of Constanza, the large harbour by the Black Sea. Lya's parents lived there and Lya's uncle Spiros was the senior practitioner of one of the neighbourhood practices and qualified to supervise the students' work. Secretly Myra hoped she would perhaps meet someone else there so her feelings for Dan would fade.

The two girls had a lovely time by the sea. They took surgery in the mornings. Myra assisted Spiros in the surgery it was her first contact with real life medical practice outside hospital, and Myra loved it. She did home visits, met the nurses and the midwives. That was what she had wanted; she felt ready.

Spiros owned a yacht. Like any Greek, his love was the sea and sailing was strong. It was seaworthy but he was not allowed to sail on the open sea. The authorities feared he could cross the Bosphorus Canal and land in Turkey. Hence, the yacht was moored on the large nearby lake, at the far end of the tourist resort of Mamaia. After the surgery closed for the day, Spiros would take the girls on the back of his motorbike and go straight to the beach. They would swim a few hours, buy some food and go and eat on the yacht. Other friends of his joined later and, as the evening fell, they sailed round the lake waiting for the night-clubs to open their doors. Spiros knew the waiters,some were his patients, and the group was allowed in, even to clubs open only for foreign tourists. Sometimes, when the moon was out, they would all go for a swim in the dark along the ray of moonlight splashed across the black sea. The next morning would be back to work. They were all young, never tired. For Myra it was a whirlwind time. She felt her feet never touched the ground. She and Lya met lots of people. They did not have much time to think of the boyfriends they had both left behind.

Dan wrote to her often, lovely letters, and after a time, Myra found herself eagerly waiting for the postman to arrive. Whenever she met another young man in among Spiros's large group of friends and acquaintances, she could not help comparing him to Dan. Each time Dan came the winner. Myra knew he had won her heart.

That late evening when the father and his son returned from Focsani, Dan knocked on Myra's window. He knew she would be awake.Yes, he said, her parents had received them well. Esther had cooked a lavish meal. And they both agreed that Myra and Dan could marry.

On that night before her wedding Myra's thoughts once again turned back. She was still troubled. Just a couple of days before the wedding Esther came to Bucharest. She brought wedding presents but she said that after a lot of soul searching she could not, just could not, face the prospect of being present to witness the marriage. She gave Myra her blessing but she could not be persuaded to stay. She left with Bea, leaving behind a trail of bitterness, Myra angry and unsettled. Her thoughts turned again to the present and the future. Myra and Dan, together they would make a good team, no matter the difficulties that lay ahead.

Here they were, on the hot day of August, linking their future- whatever that might bring.

She was now going to marry Dan.

27
TO THE VILLAGE

In the summer of 1961, newly graduated from medical school, Myra left Bucharest. She left with a few of her colleagues. They had all chosen to work out their contract – the time of penance, they called it – in the same part of the country. Their training had been free of charge and now it had to be paid for with work in a village chosen by the ministry. The new graduates had no choice. There was no alternative, no way of saying no.

Myra did not know what to expect. She was not happy, and she was not unhappy. It was the way it was and she accepted it. Mixed feelings of fear and expectation competed for attention. Deep down she knew she was taking a decisive new step into the future, a new leap for better or worse, like a her marriage a month before. It was a leap in the dark, like everything else that had happened in the last few years.

It was a break with the past. There would be no more carefree evenings listening to Paganini with Puiou and Andre or Aurore. No more wandering along the streets of Bucharest to admire the architecture of the churches. No more getting in by the back door to concerts at the Atheneum or the Opera, where for a small bribe for the porter one could sit on the steps of the gallery. No more marching along the streets chanting rude songs with a group of fellow-students, no more going into one of the famous patisseries and asking for a slice of cake and 12 teaspoons. How they all laughed to see the confusion on the salesgirl's face. No more traipsing up the mountains at weekends and busking at the train station to collect enough money for the return ticket.

Myra did not think she would miss the heavy work as a nurse at the polyclinic, or the 'voluntary' attendance at the meetings organised by the Socialist Youth Union. She was no longer a member, but kept going so that no-one would start wondering why she was not there. Nor would she miss the compulsory attendance at the processions and parades to celebrate the socialist leaders, or to mark important dates in the communist calendar – though she had a strong suspicion that such duties would still occur. So here is the future – the future Myra did not plan and she did not look forward to without apprehension.

For Myra, the country was somewhere she had never been. She was a townie, albeit from a small town, and she had lived the last six years in Bucharest, the capital city. She had spent her holidays either back home in Focsani or by the seaside at Constantza. Occasional stops at Sinaia, or at Predeal in the mountains had not enlarged her horizons much further. The only acquaintance she had with village people was at the Nation's Market in Bucharest, or the few farmers who came to the city with their baskets full of cheese, sour milk, sour cream, fruit and vegetables, carried on a pole over their shoulders – and even they had dwindled away in recent years.

Myra did not make any comment. She had by then accepted Codin's invitation to a meal at his house. She was starving and she was anxious to finish on time to catch the evening train home.

Codin's house was not far from the village church. Myra looked furtively at Codin to see if he crossed himself as they passed in front of the house of God. He did not. Therefore she did not have to sign herself, she did not have to pretend. There was a large open space in front of the church, the village green, and to the left the village shop - a small shack where a few men stood outside drinking something that smelled like plum brandy. The miasma of sour wine dregs filled the air.

Codin's house was on the mill road. It was a tidy one-storey house with the traditional wooden veranda and a neat wooden gate. On the veranda and in the windows there were pots full of geranium, bright red flowers which seemed to smile at Myra. They were the first spots of colour she had seen in the grey-brown grey village.

'Welcome.'

A plump, youngish woman greeted the arrivals at the door. She wore a brightly coloured scarf and had a high, pleasant voice like a church bell. Codin introduced her as his wife. Behind her, smiling shyly, was a second woman, much younger and very fair of skin and hair, with the palest blue eyes.

'Come forward,' Codin said to her. 'This is Lily, my daughter and my assistant. Hopefully she will become a proper nurse.'

The girl must have been still in her teens, and she had a vacant air about her. Myra said nothing, smiled and shook hands with the two women. They both quickly disappeared, leaving Codin to attend to his guest.

He guided her to the front room, the parlour, where the table, adorned with a cloth lavishly embroidered with red and black flowers in the traditional Romanian style, was set for a meal. On the walls hung shawls of the finest silk. On a day bed at the far end of the room was a thick woollen cover striped red, black and white. This lovely cheerful room was in the Romanian tradition, such as Myra had only seen before in the museum of village life in Bucharest.

'Come on, where is this the food?' Codin spoke in a loud, masterful voice, and his wife hurried in with bread and cheese and pickles. Lily followed with a bottle of red wine. She filled only three glasses, and Myra noticed there were only three places laid at the table. She asked if the wife would be joining them.

'Oh no, she is busy in the kitchen.She will eat later' said Codin. Myra thought it strange : the wife not to eat with the family. She did not think this was right but it occurred to her that villages still maintained a tradition of male dominance. The women were there to serve their men, look after the children and ate in the kitchen when they had time.

During the meal, Codin did most of the talking: about his life, how he had worked in the village since he graduated as a nurse so many years ago.

How times had changed, but not so much for him, since he was not a rich man. He just had his work and made a good living from it. He had only one child, and he wanted her to be a nurse. Politics? Changes? All that passed him by. Those were none of his business. Myra took the hint. The less said about politics, the better and she totally agreed with that.

Lily smiled. She seemed reserved and self-contained and did not say much. Myra, freshly qualified in medicine, had a passing thought that Lily looked like those children who carried a congenital condition: what with her pale colouring, very fair hair and blue eyes, but she dismissed the idea;she must not indulge in the habit of making diagnosis and labeling people every time she looked at them. Codin said that she was his one and only child. In those uncertain times, people were having fewer children.

When the meal was over, Myra said goodbye to the hostess and Codin went out to borrow a horse and cart from a neighbour.

At last, at the end of a long and exhausting day, Myra made her way back to the station and home.

29
MISGIVINGS

The journey back to Bucharest North Station took three long hours. It was a slow train which stopped at most stations : Mihaesti , Roshiori and many more. Myra could not rest on her journey home. Her mind was racing with those new messages, new facts and impressions, needing to order them in her head and reflect upon them.

Her mind kept turning to Codin. A shrewd country man. He was the one with the knowledge, the experience and deep understanding of the people and the country ways. He was one of them. He had the upper hand. For the time being. Till she found her feet, so to speak, and built her confidence. There was a lot to learn from him. She hoped she would not have to quarrel with him or the midwife.

The village? Well, Uncle John was right, it was not the best choice. She should have listened to him and gone up north of the county where orchards grew and vineyards and houses were better built and people more educated. Seaca was a poor, backward place, but how was she to have known? Her only criteria, as she saw it, was to be as near as possible to her home and her husband. It was going to be hard: no telephone, no electricity and an improvised surgery. What will be like in the middle of winter? The worrying thing was that she knew nothing of the book-keeping, or the handling of medicines; ledgers, the iventory, stock taking records were strange words with no meaning to her. She would have to ask Dan to give her some lessons. He had some training in this. Myra's thoughts then strayed to Lilly. She appeared to be a cause for worry. She seemed to be a little vague and lacking schooling yet, she was Codin's daughter. She must be careful not to be too harsh on her but at the same time should keep an eye on her.

Myra had not met the midwife but from the veiled comments, words thrown here and there during the meal, she had a feeling that there did not seem to be much love lost between the staff, nor was there much cooperation or friendship. The midwife drank too much, or so it was said, she might be lazy and was not very reliable. 'Well, we shall see.'

With those thoughts, Myra finally arrived back to Bucharest. Dan was waiting on the platform and was eager to hear her news.

Although she was almost falling off her feet from tiredness, the whole family: Silky and George and Dan and Lydia and even young Amy gathered around to hear her story. They talked long into the night.

30
HONEYMOON

The time for the delayed honeymoon had finally arrived and Myra and Dan started their preparations. They had had to postpone their plans for so long, because of Myra's need to stay put till her work placement was finalised. The other major problem was their lack of money. They had to wait till the end of the month for Dan's salary. Dan's was the only money coming in besides Silky's small contribution from her modest salary as a primary school teacher. There was never enough money to last till the end of the month, and no one to borrow from.

One day, like so many other times towards the end of the month before pay day, young Amy was sent out to buy some bread and milk with the last money left in the kitty. She returned with a bunch of flowers instead, because she liked them and they smelled nice . The row that followed...! Myra smiles at such memories.

For the much wished honeymoon, the young couple decided to accept one of Dan's aunt's invitation. She and her husband, a retired sea captain, lived in a small bungalow by the Black Sea resort of Mamaia, not far from the port of Constanza; as a wedding gift she had invited the newlyweds to spend a holiday by the sea. She had offered her guest room for their use.

Myra and Dan could not wait. They were so looking forward to the sun, the sea and the nice restful time they both needed after such intense, emotionally draining events. But their joy was cut short when Silky and George told the young couple that they too needed a holiday and saw no problem in their joining them. They had already written to aunt Flory, Silky's sister and she had no objection. That came like a bombshell to Myra, but Dan did not seem to find it unusual. He took the news calmly. He had lived with his mum and dad and his sisters all his life and this did not strike him as unnatural. Myra did not say anything and went along with their plan. She hated quarrels, particularly as this was so early in their marriage. Nevertheless, the shine had been taken off the event.

Myra spent two weeks of sun, sand and frustration. Dan seemed comfortable with the arrangement.They made love here and there when the others were elsewhere, always quietly, so as not to be overheard, but the joy of it, the discovery of new intimacies, came and went.

Doubts started to enter Myra's mind. Had it been such a wise move to get married?

Still, it was done. There was no going back, not after the family upset she had caused.

Esther had never approved, nor had she come to terms with the fact her daughter married outside her faith. To think that Esther was the one who had all those progressive ideas, who talked of assimilation and integration, who sent the girls to a non-faith school, in spite of the opposition from her own family… But when it came to the crunch she had recoiled as if a snake had bitten her. She had refused to have anything to do with Myra and had abandoned her, vowing never to take part in her future life. At Dan's and Myra's wedding, all Dan's family was there. From Myra's side only Usher came to be by his daughter's side. No Esther, no Bea.

To prove Esther right was not to be considered, not even to be thought about. Dan's family were kind people, loving and helpful. It was only that years of being on the run from persecution had made them look at life in a different way.They were used to sharing everything and expected Myra to fit in and do the same .

Myra, the young romantic, thought marrying would create a new nucleus and they would be a family with their own way of life, albeit living in close proximity to the parents. She now realised it was going be a slow process and quite an uphill struggle.

Although she still dreaded her future work assignment in the country, deep down she started to look forward to it. She hoped that there, in the God forsaken village of Seaca, she and Dan would start a life of their own as a family.

31
SETTLING IN

The first of November was Dan's birthday and they celebrated it in the village, having arrived the previous day by train. The two were laden with lots of luggage: bedding, clothes, oil lamps, a petrol small, wartime primus cooker, cooking utensils, soap, candles, matches, toilet rolls and of course, a supply of Benson and Hedges cigarettes. And, most important: Myra's newly bought stethoscope, which cost a lot of money and took a lot of trouble to find.

Codin, dressed in the same coat and floppy coarse felt hat as before, was waiting on the platform. By his side, a small, skinny man, grinning with all his protruding teeth was waiting as well. On his head he wore *a cushma*- the traditional tall lamb's fur conical hat. As soon as Myra and her husband descended from the train, the smaller man rushed forward and got hold of the luggage. Codin introduced him as Jon and both Codin and Jon took turns to kiss Myra's hand, welcoming her, and to shake hands with Dan .

'Welcome Mister Engineer,' Codin said, ramoving his battered hat. 'Can you see that hill? There are all the people that I looked after over the years.' He started laughing and expected Dan to join in the mirth.

Obviously, that was one of the most favourite jokes in Codin's repertoire, Myra thought. On the other side of the station, a cart and horse were waiting. Jon stepped forward and loaded the luggage, then he climbed into the driver's seat. Codin climbed in the back and invited Myra and Dan to sit next to him on the wooden bench.

'I hope you did not mind, Doctor,' Codin began in a soft, honey-like voice. 'I've appointed this man. He is a good, honest one, he doesn't know much about anything, but he knows how to look after a horse. Oh, I've forgotten to tell you, we were given this horse for the practice, for your home-visits. They also promised some kind of carriage to go with the horse. It hasn't arrived yet, so I have borrowed this cart from a neighbour of mine. Jon is going to do the cleaning early in the morning before we arrive at the surgery. He will light the fire, I have told him he will have to look after your fires in the winter, and also clean your house.'

'Where is that going to be?' You did not mention this the last time we spoke.' Myra said.

'I have found a room for you; you will be pleased to know it's only two houses down from the dispensary. Nice elderly people. I hope you will like it there,' he said, addressing himself mostly to Dan.

'Thank you,' Myra replied, You've taken a lot of trouble'

Myra and Dan, seated on the bench behind the driver on top of all the luggage, looked at each other. All appeared to be all right but... a horse? How was she going to deal with a horse? Back home only Usher knew about those things. She would have preferred a bike.

But on the other hand a bike would not be of much use in the thick mud or snow.

'Where is this horse going to live? And what about the food?' Dan asked.

'It is all under control, Mister Engineer. The County is sending a quota of hay and straw and grains for now and every following three months thereafter. It is all in our budget and they are going to pay Jon a salary, the rent for the dispensary, as well as for the doctor's lodgings,' Codin replied, addressing all the answers to Dan. 'As we did not have a storage place for the horse's fodder, I had it placed it in my own barn for the time being.' He was still talking to Dan as if it was he who was going to be in charge.

It wasn't long before the village materialised. Dan found a minute to whisper in Myra's ear, 'Codin looks like he is planning to feed his animals as well, for free!' Myra shrugged her shoulders briefly and said nothing. It was too much to take all this in and to worry about the horse's fodder as well.

A drizzly cold rain which had barely started when they came off the train on that November day accompanied them all through the journey, like an unwelcome guest and dampened their spirits even further. The village borrowed the colour of the weather, wearing a forloren look although it was still early in the day.

'Well, at least the dust does not clog up my lungs now,' Myra muttered to herself .

Jon did not stop at the surgery but guided the horse a few houses further along the road before halting in front of a low gate. Behind the gate and leaning on it for support, a tall elderly man with a face chiselled by years and weather lifted a hand in greeting. He left his place and turned round: 'Theodora, the town people have arrived. Come and greet them!'

A much older woman appeared in the doorway, rubbing her hands on her apron. Her head was covered in a black kerchief twisted round her head and tied in a knot at the nape of her neck. A few stray strands of grey hair escaped over her dark ears.

'Come on in, Codin, bring the Mister and Missus in!'

Codin jumped down and picked up one of the suitcases that Jon had started to unload.

'Come in Mister Engineer, these are the owners of this house, Florian and Theodora. They have agreed to rent the front room to your lady wife.' Dan looked embarrassed and turned to Myra. 'This is the Doctor who is going to live here! I only came to help my wife!' Then he turned towards Myra, half serious, half laughing: 'See what Uncle Codin has found for you?'

Myra did not reply but went straight to the old lady with her outstretched hand.. To her surprise the woman bent her head low, picked up Myra's hand and kissed it. Myra looked deeply embarrassed. The elderly man followed suit. Guided by them, the two 'grandees from the town', as they called Myra and Dan, went into the yard and climbed up a few wooden steps onto a wooden veranda which ran the length of the house. The main door opened into a whitewashed empty entrance hall through which one could catch a glimpse of a back dwelling where a fire was burning and something was boiling in a large pot black like a cauldron.

Theodora led the way, inviting the group into the front room.

'Very spacious and a large window with a wide ledge. You could put your books there,' Dan said in a low voice.

'And the gas lamp. And my radio. I should have thought of curtains. You know that large throw I had from my mother's house when I was a student, the blue one with white pattern is in the bags somewhere. Could you fix it for me?'

' There is this large stove,'Codin interrupted.

'Which one? This big bulging wall sticking out from the back wall? It has no opening.?How do I put some wood or coal in ? Or does it work with clear cold air only?

Dan stepped on Myra's foot. 'No need to be sarcastic, dear, better ask Codin.'

'Oh no. in these parts we have the hearth outside the room and we do not use wood..There isn't any round here, you may have noticed. We use straw and corn sticks, whatever comes from the fields after harvest. Only the rich landowners, now gone, used wood brought in from other parts of the country.'

'No idea how I am going to manage here; the fire, the washing, the cooking. Where will I store my things? I should have had a dowry chest. And who is going to spend hours outside to feed the fire? Not me, for sure.What a silly idea to stay and freeze outside first in order to warm up an empty room!'

'There must be a way. I would have a word with your colleagues if I were you.'

'It's easy for you to say! You going back to Mummy and Daddy in the comfort of Udrican 24, Central Bucharest!'

'Let's see how it goes first. I know you are upset.' Myra no longer said a thing in case her anger got the better of her. Why should she have to put up with all this? Nobody had asked her if she wanted to live like that. There was no training given for this. She just looked around at the uneven, whitewashed walls, at the dirt floor the colour of earth - as if the room grew out from the earth like a hollow tree. A prison, she thought, a prison with open doors but no way out. No alternative, no second choice. She agreed it was part of the contract - it was only fair that if one studied for free, one had to give something back - but this was beyond what she had ever imagined the price would be.

'Don't know how I am going to leave you here. Have you seen the kitchen?' Dan ventured.

'I expect I will see it soon enough. Whatever it is, I won't let it beat me! I'll find a way. As for the fire,' Myra turned to Codin, 'I will keep you to your word! You've said Jon should take care of this in good time, before I arrive from work. I will need to have the place clean and warm.'

'Codin is a man of his word,' he said and his posture tightened and he beat his chest with pride.

Another man came in the house before Codin had a chance to speak another word. He was a large man in his mid-forties, clad in town wear, distinctly different from the farmers' clothes. He had a booming loud voice.

'Come in, son,' old Florian said and the new arrival introduced himself.

'Emilian Rogoveanu is my name and I am the manager of the village mill,' he said, pushing his chest forward with pride. 'These are my parents. I only live next door and I have come to invite you all to my house and partake of a meal with us.'

Everybody agreed and set off through a little gate in the fence separating the two properties to the next door dwelling where a lavish dinner table was laid out in their front room. Codin walked near Jon and whispered something in his ear. Jon made his excuses and stayed outside.

Cheese, sausages, eggs, pickles and freshly baked bread made the guests' mouths water. Plum brandy was poured into small earthenware cups and everyone drank and toasted Myra's arrival.

Welcome wishes were spoken and expressions of joy at having a doctor in the village. Dan partook of the food with enthusiasm but especially of the drink. Tongues started to loosen up and jokes to fly across the table. Roast lamb followed the first course and more bread and pickles and a red heavy wine, home brewed. Myra made an effort to lighten up a bit, to share in the gaiety, but inside she felt numb. Like landing on a new planet and cautiously finding her way in.

The young couple came back to their room, and put the mattress they had brought with them on the bed that was carried in from Emilian's house. Then Jon followed with a wooden table and two wooden chairs. Myra busied herself with covering the mattress and pillows with bed linen. It was chilly and Dan covered the floor with a jute carpet. He put a few of their wedding photos on the wall and the books on the window-sill.

It all looked almost homely, what with the radio transmitting light music and Doina Badea and Margareta Paslaru, the fashionable singers they both loved, singing Myra's favourite tunes.

The next morning they went to inspect the kitchen. It was a most primitive place at the back of the house with two fire earth facing each other. One was lit and warm, the other cold. In between the two stood a three legged low round table surrounded by several milking stools. Theodora was sitting on one of the stools in front of the lit fire, cooking a large polenta in the black cauldron that Myra had noticed the previous day. The cauldron was hanging on a hook suspended by a chain just above the fire.A smaller pot full of milk was bubbling in a recess of the fireplace. A smell of yeast and dough came from a wooden pail placed on a higher level in another deep brick shelf above the fire and further from it. The roof of this kitchen was half built and half open, covered with a canopy made out of thick cloth.

Tudora kept stirring the polenta mixture with a large wooden spoon. She let it bubble gently till it became hard like a cake thick batter. Then she removed the cauldron from the fire and with a deft movement overturned its contents on to the wooden table where the creamy yellow hot, soft mass slipped out and formed what looked like a large pudding. She took the empty pot, filled it with water from a pitcher, emptied onto the earthen floor then filled it with milk and returned it to the fire. Theodora put earthenware bowls round the table and poured hot milk into each then ladled polenta into each bowl. .Breakfast was ready.

'Do you think you could manage to do something like that?' Dan asked, barely able to control a laugh.

'I may, but in the meanwhile I will ask Theodora to do it. Then I'll start cooking on my little gas stove. Just like my mother used to do it during those war years. After all, I watched her long enough.'

'Good!'

'And I shall ask Codin what he meant about not worrying about cooking,' she continued. After that, Myra wanted to find out about the rest of the facilities and Codin cracked another one of his classic jokes.

'You know how it is around here for the toilet, Doctor? It's a hole in the ground and two pillars, one to hold on to, the other to keep the flies and dogs away!' It was almost true,–as they were to find out later. There was a cabin, and a cut out seat onto an upturned wooden box. The cabin, which was at the bottom of the yard, had a door but it failed to close. Luckily, there were better facilities three doors down at the surgery. It reminded Myra of the outside toilet sthey had at the bottom of their home garden when she was a little girl. She went once there all by herself and fell in and smeared her coat and Mama was angry. A bucket was another item to be brought from Bucharest and Dan dutifully added it to his list (not to mention more toilet paper!). Dan was due to leave the next day as it was a Sunday, and he was due back at work on Monday.

Jon presented himself to take Dan to the station early next morning. To everybody's surprise he came along in an old battered hackney carriage with the horse in harness. The black, imposing hackney was delivered for Myra's use, with the compliments of the regional authority. Jon had apparently spent all night cleaning it and mending it a little, ready for use. Codin and Emilian came to say their goodbyes. Dan left, driven by Jon, to catch his train with almost the whole village watching.

After his departure Codin and Emilian turned to Myra and said, 'What a fine husband you have Doctor; he can drink plum brandy by the tankard just like us!'

Well Myra thought, I'm glad that Dan was a hit but that was not a reason I ever considered for marrying him!

32
MANAGEMENT

Myra spent her first night alone and it was a cold, dark and lonely one. The following day the medical practice began. A truck brought the supply of medicines, equipment, a portable gas stove and everything else necessary. Myra signed the receipt for the whole delivery and spent the rest of the day checking each item, writing it in the newly provided ledger and, with Codin's help, placing every item in the cupboards. They started an inventory and Myra sent Jon to buy a padlock. It was agreed she would be the only one to have the keys and an emergency bag would be left for Codin's use in her absence. There was: penicillin in vials for injections; streptomycin in bottles, the powder to be reconstituted with water for injections; glass syringes of different sizes and steel needles, each with rods for cleaning them inside; a gas balloon and a burner with a simple sterilizing unit; powders of piramidon (paracetamol was as yet unknown), aspirin, digoxin tablets in various sizes and ampoules; quinine, aspirin, suppositories for children, various instruments, a mercury sphygmomanometer for measuring blood pressure, a microscope and a set of tubes for checking different blood tests and litmus paper. There were also bandages and dressings, forceps scissors, even obstetric forceps. Large bottles of ether, morphine and tablets of codeine had to be locked separately. With the horse, the fodder and all those medical things,Myra felt suddenly burdened by a lot of responsibility - not to mention the hackney carrriage. Myra remembered wistfully, the carriages that could be hired in Bucharest for an outing on the boulevard through the triumphal arch. It was a great pitty, she thought that the medical training did not include accountancy and bookkeeping. She only hoped Codin and the midwife would turn out to be honest people that she could trust and with whom she could share the responsibility. As for Jon, he took up his new role with great pride sitting in the driver's seat so the whole village would notice him and look up to him.

Myra made some of her first decisions. She sent Codin to the parish hall to ask for a stove and a second gas burner for the sterilization of the larger pieces of equipment. He did not object; in fact he seemed to say: ' All right, Doctor,' to everything she asked. That was a good start. Or was it? Then Myra plucked up enough courage to say that she would prefer the horse's fodder to be stored at the surgery. She told him that she had already spoken with the owners and that Mr Nitzulescu has agreed to let her use their silo. Jon looked at Codin, waiting for a reaction, but Codin said nothing, just bowed his head in agreement. If he did not like it, he did not show it. The problem of the hackney storage was then discussed. Myra sent Codin to negotiate with the other Nitzulescu brother across the divide, and it was agreed that they could leave the hackney on his side of the yard. There was such good will all around!

Jon came every morning to feed the horse, harness it, clean, and start the fires ready for the day's work. Consultations had to take place in daylight only.

It soon became obvious that Lily was rather clumsy and when trusted to do the simplest tasks on her own, no matter how many times she was shown what to do it, all went wrong. Codin was appeared to be aware of the situation but did not say anything and discretly took over most of the duties allocated to his daughter. Myra pretended she had not noticed and instead she gave Lilly simple jobs like cleaning the needles with the rods after use and sterilizing the instruments after surgery. She was pleased to do the job and be trusted. She was a sweet, obedient girl but Myra had noticed she was living in fear of her father. God only knew how she was treated at home.

Little by little people started to drift in. At first they came out of curiosity but then, they started to talk, seeing that Myra listened to their complaints and did not make any judgements.. Codin took it upon himself to do a sort of 'triage' of what was urgent and what was not and what was likely to be infectious. Myra approved and felt relieved that he was doing the right thing without being told. However, through the thin partition wall she could hear Codin greeting the people at the door. Her right eyebrow started to rise when she heard him asking: 'What have you got? No, not what you came for. I mean, what have you brought in the satchel? Did you think to bring a little gift for the doctor?' Most of them came prepared with some eggs, fresh bread or cheese, even a bottle of plonk, all home-made. Some, however, did not bring anything and Myra could hear Codin telling them off:

'Aren't you ashamed of yourselves? To come empty handed to the doctor, who learned so many years and came specially for you from Bucharest to look after you?' Myra was incensed; How dare he make such statements without permission? She had to have words with Codin.

After surgery, when the last patient was out of hearing, Myra asked Codin, the midwife and Lily to stay behind. She expressed her discontent and insisted such practices were unwelcome and dangerous. Both Codin and the midwife protested, saying that was the custom of the land and Myra should not interfere. Myra said that times had changed and old practices had to be put to rest. It was not the thing to do, people were entitled to free medical care. They both replied that was how they lived round here, everybody did the same for the vicar who visited once a month for service or weddings and funerals and even the mayor received offerings in return for favours.

Myra pointed out that complaints might reach the ears of the Party reps.

'Even the old Gypsy woman who was consulted by the people to keep the evil eye away from them or cure their beasts got offerings and gifts,' said the midwife. Why ever not her?

Nobody ever complained. So Myra had to become resigned to leave things as they were. At least she managed to get a promise from her staff not to tell the people off on her behalf, if they were coming empty handed. Lilly said nothing; her mind seemed to be floating away from everyday reality. Codin bowed his head low and promised, for his part, no longer to ask for gifts. Obviously he was worried about his income diminishing. After that, when he arranged the home visit, he shrewdly scheduled it in such a way, to make sure at least one of the visits ended up at lunch time and an invitation to eat with the patient's family followed. And, miraculously, the dinner was ready and the table. Myra started to understand this man: whatever task he was given he would say yes, then find a way to do it the way he wanted.

33
FLORIAN'S STORY

The light faded with the advancing winter at about 3pm and the consulting room had to close. It was cold and grey even by daylight. And it was cold in Myra's room at home. There was never enough time for Jon to spend feeding the fire. It was warmer in Theodora's room as she started cooking early and the stove on her side and kept the fire burning. Jon was free to see to Myra's stove only after he had finished his duties at the surgery, also after he had driven her in the resplendent carriage to visit her patients. Myra wondered what the country folks thought, seeing her tiny figure in the large carriage passing by. What was more hilarious was that the horse was an elderly animal, well set in his ways, as they soon discovered. He liked to return to his new home at the surgery once he reached his destination and stopped for a while. No matter how hard Jon, or even Codin, tried to make him continue his journey from one place to the next, the horse would not move. He would only turn round and go back home. If another visit was required, they had to start again from the surgery. This forward – and back repeated journey took an awful lot of time and caused a lot of merriment in the village. It was the same at the main crossroads. Luckily, the village had only two major intersections, because at each of the crossroads the horse would turn round and head for home. It was evening by the time all the visits were completed and Myra returned to her room and she found it slightly warmer as the inner bricks had had time to warm up. Either because of that or Myra no longer felt the cold because at each home she visited, she was treated, as the custom was, with a glassful of the local home-brewed wine, which one could not refuse out of fear of insulting and antagonizing the patient's family. Armed with between four and seven glasses of wine and very little food – only the pickles offered with the wine or a piece of bread – Myra no longer noticed the cold so much. She would only stagger in, go and say hello to the Rogoveanus, then retire to her room to sleep it all off. She had warned Theodora to check that she did not fall asleep with a cigarette still burning. The nights were not going to be quiet for long. First it was Florian Rogoveanou, who seemed to spend most of the nights outside. Unless it was raining heavily or snowing outside, he will be propped up at the gate sighing and coughing a thick chesty cough. Then he would pace up and down along the wooden veranda. It was months later that Myra discovered the secret of his night wanderings.

Myra wondered if Florian ever slept. Her thoughts turned to Theodora. What sort of a life did she have? Once she asked her why Florian was so restless at night? All she answered was: 'Silly old fool!' Then some nights were disturbed by the couple's son. The charming, hospitable Emilian liked to drink and every so often would get very drunk. The first thing he would do when staggering home late at night the worse for wear, was to start hurling abuse at every one and to beat his poor gentle wife, Lyna. Myra's heart tightened in her chest many a night when she was awakened from sleep by the running steps of Lyna and her children who sought refuge at her in-laws. When Emilian was in that state, the only one who could calm him down was his father, Florian. The following day, Emilian would wake up with a sore head and go to the mill oblivious of what havoc he had caused during the night, not having the slightest recollection of the pain he had inflicted on his wife and children. Poor Lyna, so plump and gentle, and the wonderful, clever daughters. What life was that; night after night going to sleep, not knowing when they will be waked up by shouting and blows, Lyna would wake them up from their sleep and drag them out in the night across the fence to seek refuge with their grandparents? Did they talk to anyone about this? What did they say at school? It did not seem to affect their learning. Both were top of their class and had made plans to go to university. Myra visited them often and helped them with their French homework. The two were so eager to learn, to better themselves, yet their acceptance of their lot in life was total. Nobody contemplated divorce or separation. No neighbour or relative would intervene, except for Emilian's father who, in his kind, quiet way talked to his son. And that burly, aggressive son stood with his head down, not uttering a single word in front of his father. Then for a while it would be peace and quiet and

236

everybody got on with their lives. Till next time. One time Myra discreetly approached the midwife on the subject without giving any names. She had learned by that time that the midwife was a frightful gossip. The midwife told her a most amazing story. From then on, out of curiosity Myra payed more attention to what was going on as the evening fell.

When Florian would reposition himself at the gate under cover of darkness, Myra was waiting to see if Margaret, the widow who lived across the road, would come out on her porch talking to the neighbours on the other side of her fence or to the hens and ducks that she was feeding. The minute that she finished her jobs and she would go in and Florian would give a loud sigh. After a while, Margret would come out again having changed her blouse for a finer one, all embroidered, and a floral scarf on her head and beads around her neck, and take a chair by her gate and sit turning her head this way and that, taking in the fresh evening air. Indoors, Theodora would be preparing the evening meal. When it was ready she would call Myra and Florian to dinner. After a repeated call she would give up on Florian, and Myra and Theodora share a meal in silence. Piece by piece, Myra learned and understood.

This is Florian's story, in his own words:

My name is Florian. I should be a happy man with such a name, fresh and full of stamina. But that was not to be. I spend long nights pacing up and down the long wooden veranda smoking. Smoking and walking, waiting in case she shows up. I want to see her in the

237

early hours of the morning when she wakes up to feed the hens, when she lifts and carries the wooden pails on her still slender shoulders. At night I watch her window across the road and wait for the light. Sometimes she shows up, sometimes not. She likes to tease me, to punish me, to remind me constantly of the wrong I have done her.

'Come in man, you'll catch your death!' My wife Theodora's voice grates on my ears.I cannot listen to her croaky voice, her mumbling. I light a roll-up and drag deep. The cough is overpowering so that the sound of her is drowned. After a while, Theodora gives up and then I can stop walking and lean on my gate and wait. Wait and sigh. Wait and smoke the cheroot that is slowly killing me. Her name, which I repeat without break in my mind and murmur voicelessly with my lips, is Margret. The night is falling at the blink of an eye. I watch her saying good night to her friends before turning in. She never looks my way although she knows I am here. Her window turns from dark to yellow gold. I wait to see her shadow. Sometimes she draws the curtains and sometimes not. I see her shadow in front of the window as though she is looking out at the night. Perhaps she is looking at me. She knows I am here, she knows I love her and that my love has never faded. She slowly removes her headscarf. She wore black after her husband died, and now she changed it. She starts uncoiling her hair from the tight plait that crowns her head. Oh, how I wish I could do that again, when her hair was shiny and soft under my fingers, rough from work. I can still smell the hay tangled in her hair as it was when we made love in the loft full of hay. She lingers by the window, a dark shape combing

her hair and starting to undress, slowly removing her garments one by one. Oh, Daisy how can you still punish me so? In all those years we followed the paths in life that God has ordered for us, you never found forgiveness in your heart and I never found peace. We were so young forty years ago. Barely sixteen, I used to spy on you hidden behind the bushes by the river, waiting for you, the prettiest girl of our village to show up with your washing or to gather jute and wash the stems in the fast flowing waters, all the time laughing and singing with your friends. You used to carry the laundry basket on your head, kneel by the river , lift your white shirt to pin it up by your tiny waist and tuck it into the belt of your woolly skirt.I used to get so hot and bothered seeing your round behind moving rhythmically as you rubbed the cloth to and fro. From time to time you would look back as if you knew I was watching. On your way back, somehow, as if missing the path where all the other women walked, you came near where I was hidden, almost brushing against me with your skirt while still chatting with your friends.Then one day as in a dream my will was overpowered by my desire and I stretched a hand without knowing what I was doing and grabbed your skirt. I knew then you felt the same about me. You did not swear or scream in anger, but slowly lowered your hand and touched mine, removing it gently from your skirt. Then you ran and caught up with your friends. I stayed there kissing my own hand where it had touched you. I ran back to the fields.

It was the harvest time then and all hands were needed. I hoped my father hadn't noticed I was gone for such a long time. He had already given me some of his sermons and warnings.But he lifted his head from the lane of golden corn with glaring eyes. I knew he knew. I pulled my hat down over my eyes and carried on cutting at the corn. I worked much faster than he did. I was young and strong then. We were a poor family and I was the only son. We worked for the landowner whom we had never met but we lived in fear of the overseer. He was the bailiff who counted all the rows we had done in a day and worked out our pay. We were not even tenants and had but a small piece of land of our own. I hacked at the long stems in anger for all the time I wished I was near you. I counted the hours till I could sneak down by the river and wait for you. The way you moved, your strength and the graceful way you cut the tall rushes, your singing, were all in my head. And when one day you strayed off the path again and let me squeeze your warm hand and whisper to meet you at the cowshed - that was my blessed moment. We climbed in the hay loft and kissed and fondled and swore to love each other for ever. I gave you a little cross I had carved for you as I was deft with my hands.You wore it from that moment on a ribbon round your neck.

By that time the whole village knew we were sweethearts. My father though, thought otherwise. He wanted me, with my good looks and strength to lift us out from our poverty. The bailiff had a daughter, a spinster as old, perhaps, as mother. The bailiff wanted her wed and hinted to my father that he was going to settle good land and cows and a few goats on her as a dowry and build a house for the newlyweds. He told me I was to marry Theodora. It was agreed; they shook hands. I was not yet 18. No matter how I tried to reason with my father - my mother's eyes were red from crying - his word was law. I was weak and I was frightened of him and of what the bailiff could do to your family as well as mine, for your lot was as poor as ours. My father's will prevailed. When I had gathered enough courage to come and see you on a Sunday after church and told you, you stood still but for a minute and laughed loud in my face. You said no matter, you had never loved me and there were so many others to choose from. When the war started I did not wait for the call to arms. I volunteered. I was a married man, a man whose heart was dead and hoped the war would kill me. The thought of not having to watch the dark face of my wife or to feel her bony body next to me in bed egged me on.

I remember how before leaving I went to say goodbye to you. It was another Sunday and the sun had come out after many days of rain. You, as beautiful as usual, your hair I used to touch hidden under a white fine cloth, chatting by the porch with the other women, the wool, fluffy and light, tucked at your chest, your deft fingers twisted the spindle round and round and turned it into yarn. I stopped in front of you, trembling, my kepi in my hands. Sweat soaking my new tunic and I said, 'I am off to war. I came to say goodbye and to see you once more. I'll always love you!' I shouted as you turned your back to me and walked back indoors. You walked away, head held high. I felt so small then. All the other women were watching in silence. I turned and ran.

I did not die in battle. I tried hard, I was the first to rush forward in the face of danger. I smoked and smoked. I came home on leave half way through the war *and did my manly duties by my wife. Theodora was a quiet woman, hard working and quietly spoken. She never crossed me once. I got the news: Margret was to get married to Zamphyr, the smith. He was older than you were, much older than me. I could not wait to go back to the front, to Russia. I was demobbed in '44 and when I came home my son was one year old. Theodora waited until I returned to have him christened. The dark thing who got his mother's looks, we called Emilian. I did not pay much attention to him, although he turned out to be a good son. I left the care of him to his mother, as I had all heavy work and the running of the house. The old heartache and sadness all came back when I found out that your husband built a house on the plot of land just across the road from us. It was your wish and he gave in to it. It was your revenge, Margret, and ever since I have spent my life gazing at you and thinking of my loss. One thing, though, cheers me up when from time to time I glimpse the small wooden-cross still hanging round your neck.*

The cough woke Myra up and when it finally abated, sleep was gone. She got out of bed and looked outside through the window.The light at Margret's was still on but as she watched, two arms drew the curtains together. The window blackened and Myra heard Florian moving away from the gate. His steps made the wood squeak and he finally went to bed still sighing. Indoors, Theodora, deep asleep, was snoring loudly. From time to time she uttered some words. Myra did not know if she was awake or still asleep.

'Come on, man! Don't you ever settle? For Goodness sake!'

At daybreak she was up. She went out, unfastened the chain with its bucket and let it unravel down into the well. The well was deep and narrow the chain clanged. All that noise was too much for Myra. She had to get up. She washed her face with fresh water from the well and brushed her teeth. She watched how Theodora brushed her teeth with her finger and used salt instead of toothpaste Myra thought perhaps that was the best way, seeing that Theodora, at her age had all her teeth, white and strong. 'Better than mine,' she thought. Feeding the hens came next and gathering the eggs. Not many but enough for the three of them. Theodora poured the water she had brought from the well into the cauldron and then she lit the fire. While the water was boiling she sat herself on the little chair and started chopping all leftover potatopeel, cabbage, stale bread and cold polenta, all for the pig, which lived in his pen behind the house. Then the long journey to the toilet started. Theodora walked in front of Myra touching the top of the vines, checking for rot and other pests or insects as she moved forward. It looked as though she did not the need to find a toilet. She just parted her legs when she was ready and a long stream of urine came out from under her skirt. Blast! said Myra soundlessly and slowed down to avoid being splashed. 'This is disgusting,' she thought. Theodora continued walking without slowing her progress and when she had finished, she calmly lifted her white long shirt with the embroidered border and wiped herself underneath . 'Charming!' At the same time Myra was crossing her legs, which was difficult to do while at the same time trying to avoid the trail of wet left on the narrow path. She finally reached the cabin. The door did not lock and she had to hold it with one hand. And the flies! It was just as Codin had said. She ran back to the house as soon as she could leaving all that, intent on having another wash. It didn't improve her spirits at the start of a new day. Theodora, totally unaware of the reaction she had caused was already in busy preparing breakfast. Myra decided to find an excuse and leave without food. On her way in, she noticed Florian fast asleep on the veranda, his head covered by his rough coat and all around him cigarette butts from his all-night smoking. Myra smiled to herself, a smile mixed with bitterness. On one hand, she felt sorry for the poor weak sod but at the same time she despised him and felt sorry for Theodora, living her life so obviously rejected. But it was not her business how those folk lived their life. Life was cruel sometimes. No reason to get sentimental, she was there to do a job and the sooner she left the better.

34
THE FIRST AUTUMN

No excuse was needed to skip breakfast; Codin was already waiting. There was an emergency call, a young woman had been having bad pains in her abdomen all night. Her husband said she was pregnant. Codin said he had sent word to the midwife about it. Together they climbed into the hackney and drove off. Myra found the woman greatly distressed by pain and there was blood, fresh running blood. There was a hard, tender lump on the left side of her tummy. 'This is more like an ectopic,' Myra thought. As any means means of precise diagnosis was lacking and the woman was in great danger, Myra decided to send her to the hospital. It was 28 kilometres to the nearest hospital and with the roads in the state they were, it would take hours. There was no ambulance available; Codin found this out after he spent a lot of precious time walking to the parish hall to telephone. There was no other way but for the young husband to take her in the cart and horse. Myra gave her some morphine to ease the pain and off they went. It was an ectopic and she survived, as they found out much later.

There was another call at the other end of the village, but the horse would not budge. Every attempt to make him move was hopeless. Jon talked to him, pulled him by the reins, nothing. He would only head back to the surgery. So they had to go back. By that time Myra had just had a glass of wine and a slice of bread at a patient's house. At the surgery the people had started gathering but there was still time to do the visit. They would have to wait a little longer. Lily was instructed to run a triage: all rashes and fevers to wait indoors, all others to wait outside. The way to Shotinga, the hamlet attached to the main village, ran though a narrow muddy lane full of ruts. It took more than half an hour to reach that poorest side of the village. The eight month old was burning with high fever and his breath was uneven. He sucked his chest in and out, for air. His lips were blue; his skin turned a shade of grey. Myra convinced the mother to remove all the woolly wraps, and to wash him down with tepid water. Where was the steam tent, the oxygen, the perfusion she had access to at the hospital? All she had learned was in vain here. It was a long road to the nearest hospital. The baby wouldn't survive the journey.She gave him a shot of penicillin and asked the mother to bring in a bowl of hot water to have some steam in the room. The baby's weak whimper was almost inaudible. The mother knew that the father had already gone in search off the priest. An elderly woman came in with glasses full of wine and this time Myra drank it in one gulp. She then left and on her way back to the surgery she dropped Codin at the Town hall to try again for an ambulance. He had to jump down so as not to stop the carriage. At the surgery a long queue was waiting. She walked into the consulting room and the remainder of the day began.

People of all ages came to the surgery. Myra had already made it clear that she could not accommodate too many people at once in the small room, so they came in one by one. The relatives had to wait outside.They came with various ailments: loads of bad chests with bronchitis, mostly among the elderly. Dust inhalation, heavy smoking of heavy tobacco, fumes from the open fires and pollen from the fields all contributed to the dreadful situation. Tuberculosis, or the damaged lungs from the disease earlier in childhood made still people suffer. There were cases of pellagra and malnutrition among the poor and a high number of heart conditions at different stages of progression as a result of rheumatic fever. There were middle age women who felt 'faint in the heart' and Myra had to guess what exactly that meant. There were women who wanted children and women who did not want to have children because they could not feed them. Since part of the land had been taken away from the landowners by the State Agricola Farm the women had to go to work in the fields like the men, for a salary. The plot left to them could not feed more children. Large numbers of children had rickets and stunted growth and infectious childhood illnesses, among which diphtheria and scarlatina and whooping cough were still killers. New cases of smallpox and tuberculosis were rare due to a massive program of vaccination and mass surveillance. Chest X-rays and blood tests for detecting syphilis were required before applying for a job, before applying for a licence to marry. Malaria was on the decrease since the massive program of cleansing the stagnant marshes undertaken immediately after the war but tetanus was still a dread and so were polio and whooping cough and flu. Rheumatic fever left some children crippled for life and cared for by their extended families.

The winter was just beginning to show its strength with ground frost and early darkness and although Christmas was no longer mentioned officially, the feel of it was in the air. Theodora was cooking mostly vegetarian dishes, haricot beans, lentils, potatoes for the fast during the six weeks before Christmas, Hence the advent of the slaughter of the pigs, just before Christmas on St Ignatius day. Pigs were slaughtered, sheep were killed and their fur put to dry to be turned into pelts.

Earlier, in October the grapes, tiny red fruit, sweet and full of seeds, were picked from the back gardens vines and put in large metal or wooden pails. The few wine-presses owned by the villagers had to be relinquished to the State Farm so, with the exception of a one or two hidden away, the villagers rolling up their trousers had to go back to the ancient practice of dancing barefoot in the tubs and squash the grapes to squeeze the heart out of them. The red liquid stained the hands and feet and white rolled up long johns turned purple red at the lower ends. Every house turned to having a party, there was merryment with neighbours gathering at each other's houses, the red, sweet juice turning their heads. It was forbidden by law to produce plum brandy and the alembics for double distilling the alcohol were forbidden but that did not seem to stop anyone. Once the harvest of the plums was done they got busy. After all, what were they going to do with the plums? Jam and marmalade were not on their menu.

At the pig slaughter parties barbecues were lit, new wine filled the glasses and the whole village smelled of pork cracklings and grilled meat. The women were hard at work cleaning guts, mincing meat and fat adding spices and garlic, to fill yards and yards of sausage skins: thin ones, thick ones and black puddings made with the animals blood. Ham was put to dry in straw baskets and others were smoked and the fat melted and large jars filled with leftover cuts of meat, to be stored for the   winter.

It went without saying that there always was a nice cut of meat put aside for the doctor, the nurse, Codin and the midwife. Myra watched in wonder that frenzy of activities and worried how could she carry home all her new wealth of meat, wine and bread.

35
BUCHAREST FOR NEW YEAR

Three months or so since this new job started, the Chief Medical Officer, Doctor Pica, organised a meeting which took place at the hospital. It was a chance to get to know all the doctors who worked in the same area a little better, and also for Doctor Pica to read out directives from the Ministry of Health and the tasks set out for the coming year by the Socialist Party and its Government. A decree was passed that infant mortality, which was running at the time at more than 10%, was to be reduced to under 5% for the first two years then below in the following years. The doctors would be personally accountable for each infant death and would have to explain what measures they had undertaken to prevent it. A new government organisation was set up to oversee the process with powers to fine and dismiss doctors who were not achieving the set target. There was no mention of any contributions the government was prepared to put in place in order to improve child care, no new maternity units, were planned, no new equipment, no benefits for women in the villages to provide them with better nutrition, no milk distribution in schools and electricity was still not available in every village. While women working in factories or offices in towns had a right to paid medical leave, antenatal care and maternity leave, there was nothing for the farmers. However, at the meeting nobody raised any questions about whether there were any local proposals or plans for some improved facilities like incubators, oxygen stations, easy access to blood transfusions outside the hospitals. Nobody asked how many new ambulances were to be bought for improving access. Myra kept quiet like everybody else, counting in her mind how many live births she had registered in Seaca that last year. There were about thirty, perhaps thirty five. That meant that no more than three could die in the following year.

After the meeting Doctor Pica invited a few colleagues including Myra, to a private party at his house. His wife Anna was also a doctor working as a paediatrician in a village not far from Myra's. Myra was curious to meet her. The midwife in Seaca had eagerly told her all the gossip some time ago. Anna was Jewish. She had married the chief at the end of her first year at the practice where Nicou Pica worked as a new doctor. They fell in love. She got pregnant, but he was reluctant to marry her. Abandoned and depressed Anna tried to comit suicide. That made him reconsider and ' it brought him to the altar.' He was a party member, on the point of getting the job of Chief Medical Officer and a scandal had to be avoided. They had a little girl. At the party Myra met her, a delightful two year old and her mother and father seemed to get on. The party went very well. Anna proved to be a wonderful cook. In the privacy of the home the guests felt it was easier to express some of the concerns they all had. Even the hosts had some worries about the work and the way they lived. There was a good atmosphere of camaraderie. Myra, normally shy, in a spurt of enthusiasm invited all her colleagues and their partners to a New Year's Party in Bucharest and to her surprise everyone accepted. She telephoned home from the hospital and all the family were delighted, Dan eager to meet all the crowd. Only the Picas stayed behind. They celebrated the New Year in the village. It appeared that their respective parents were not accepting their marriage and they were not welcome with either of them. Anna said it was difficult to travel with their little girl but this was a feeble excuse, Myra thought. She felt a deep kinship with Anna - after all, they were in the same boat.

The journey home to Bucharest was as impatiently awaited by Myra, who was looking forward to a return to civilisation, as it was by Dan and his family. At the time, Bucharest was starving; there were queues for everything: bread, milk, eggs, matches, toilet paper, coffee and much else. The queuing often ended in disappointment. After hours of standing up in the cold, people were being sent away with empty hands as the shelves were empty. Then the poor people would rush to another shop where it was rumoured there were still products available. It took hours and a member of a family, usually a retired member or a housewife, had to dedicate his or her time to that purpose alone, otherwise people who went to work would end up with nothing to feed their families. No wonder Dan, his father, and even his mother were waiting like a reception committee on the platform for the train's arrival. What Myra wanted was a decent bath, a soak in warm water in a pleasantly warm room, and to wash her clothes in the washing machine, have her hair done, go out to see a film at the Scala Cinema or go to the 'Melody Bar and Cabaret,' which had initially been opened for foreigners only but recently had began to accept local people.The prices were so high that all Myra and Dan and their friends could afford was a small glass of Dubonnet and a big glass of mineral water which they nursed till the early hours of the morning. Myra was happy to telephone and have a chat with her friends, to feel warm and to wear nice clothes and shoes instead od heavy boots.

What was missing was news from home. There had been no communication since the wedding. She would send them a New Year's card. To look at the shops,, and especially the bookshops, was like heaven. Sometimes the group of friends would go to the theatre or the Operetta or to the Athenaeum for a concert. Cultural activities were about the only thing affordable, the arts being heavily subsidised by the state. The restaurants offered music and dance, although food was not always guaranteed. The menus contained long lists of savoury dishes but when you asked the waiter for your choice, the answer often was: 'We did have it but it's finished.' This sentence came to be the national joke - it is but it's finished. If one promised the waiter a substantial bribe though, one fared a little better; suddenly they remembered there was some food left, 'but only for you because you are so nice.'

At home, Myra was treated like a welcome guest. They all made a great effort to make her stay as pleasant as possible. There was plenty of good will but everyone was preocupied; conversations took place on different levels. The stories of one were of little interest to the others. Even Dan appeared not to take a real interest in her account of events, nor did she follow everything he said of his daily life. Myra felt somehow removed from their life as if the four of them in Bucharest spoke a different language, the language of everyday urban life, of work, who they met or spoke to or was new in the capital. They talked about working overtime, about people she didn't know, telephone conversations which didn't make sense out of context, committee meetings with the party reps, intrigues and gossip, who they suspected to be an informer, what news they heard from listening to Free Europe in secrecy, problems with the boiler and the heating and the administration's incompetence. They spoke about how many hours it took George to queue for bread. It was all as remote as possible from Myra's rural life, her fight to keep warm, her anxiety over the security of the medicines cabinet, that with the winter coming she was running out of fodder for the horse and that his the stables was inadequate; concern for her patients and her loneliness. All their problems passed her by as many of Dan's problems passed her by. She did not have a say in the day to day running of the house, which she realised by now, could not be called home yet. But everyone in the family took her into their confidence, unburdening their discontent with each other and asking Myra to sit in judgement and take sides. Lydia was bitterly complaining of the conflict with her father who was against her boyfriend to whom she was devoted. She wanted to leave home, with Myra's help if possible. Silky was unhappy with George, who was not contributing enough to the running of the house, nor was he concentrating on his writing. Amy was complaining of her mother, who made her work hard at school, which she disliked and she wanted to run away. Myra just listened and followed Dan's preference to let them fight their own battles. So, these problems passed her by, while always at the back of her mind was the nagging thought that she had left Codin alone in Seaca to run things. It did not reassure her when early one Sunday morning she was woken by the telephone. It was Codin. He sounded cheerful, most likely he was tipsy. 'Codin, where are you? Is everything allright, or has something happened?'

'I am at the village hall. I rang to inform you that as soon as you left we received a visit from high up. There was a chap from the Regional Authority with one man from Public Health, Dr Pica our chief and the party boss.' Myra's breath quickened and her heart started to beat faster but before she could say anything Codin continued: 'They inspected five bottles of wine and two bottles of plum brandy, a load of pork chops gratefully donated by Emilian and we came out 'tops' regarding our medicines, the files and the admin.! We gave them a couple of bottles each to take away to ensure our success.' Myra did not know whether to laugh or cry. She hoped nobody was around in the parish hall to hear him.

The New Year's party was a great success. All the new friends came with their wives and partners; there was plenty of wine and roast meat and cakes and a lot of dancing and jokes. Village life was a million miles away. Myra's parents-in-law were present and they taught the younger generation how to dance the Charleston. Everyone had a go, to great amusement and prizes were given to the best. And the best prize of all was that Myra got a card from her parents and sister and they all signed their names, including Esther.

The New Year celebrations over, Myra returned to the village with overwhelming feelings of unease. The winter frost started to bite. She brought all the winter clothes that she could gather: heavy boots, trousers, woolly hats and gloves. The feeling of not belonging anywhere accompanied her everywhere. She was upset to leave Dan behind, and the comfort of home, however she was glad to have a rest from the constant impact of the house full of people with their problems and their bickering. She felt somehow not needed at home and she was eager to return to the village where she was expected. But having to cart clothes and objects from one place to another, never finding what she needed in the right place at the right time made her more unsettled. The train finally reached Mihaesti station where Codin was waiting.

36
DIPHTHERIA

At first there was one sore throat among all the colds and coughs that winter usually brought. Within hours the child, a sturdy seven year old, was fighting for breath. Myra examined his throat and the tell-tale signs were there: white, thick membranes covered the tonsils, advancing speedily and threatening to obstruct the air passages. Myra asked Codin to show her his records to see if the child had received his diphtheria vaccine but files were so untidy it was impossible to be sure.

'Of course, Doctor, none of them escaped Codin,' he said, narrowing his eyes and pushing his chest forward. That was not a promising sign, by that time Myra learned to recognise when he was lying. The mother did not know or could not remember. There was no time to lose, the boy was fighting for air with all his ribs and muscles. Soon he would be exhausted and stop. Myra went to the Parish Hall to telephone Dr Pica. He did not seem surprised. In confidence, he said that they had admitted to the hospital two cases of diphteria that very day, but he had been advised to keep it quiet. They were awaiting instructions from the Regional Officer. The ambulance arrived an hour later without oxygen, but at least the child was alive and he was taken to the hospital. The next day the regional infection control medic paid them a visit. By that time a few more cases had appeared. He asked Codin to show him the record books. According to the records, a fair number of the children had missed out on the vaccine. Codin said they all had been vaccinated but sometimes he did not have time to write it in the book. He explained that the vaccine only came once a year in the spring and all the children over six months of age were called to be immunised. As the directives indicated, if a child was four or five months old he had to receive the vaccine the following year. Myra, out of loyalty, also from fear that some of the consequences would also affect her, interrupted to emphasise that such a child was by then sixteen, seventeen months old and immunity from the mother gone, giving him plenty of opportunities to get ill. Besides, spring was a busy time for the peasants and many children were left in the care of the grandparents, who did not always respond to the call. It did not help Codin or the midwife, the medic had to punish someone and report he had taken appropriate measures and they got a heavy fine. By that time, another school child had fallen critically ill. When Myra arrived he was already turning blue and his rasping short intake of breath spelt immediate danger. Myra thought how lucky she was to have spent six month of her surgical training in a hospital that specialised in upper chest and neck surgery. She had assisted her tutor on several occasions to perform a tracheotomy.

'Doctor, you can't do it on your own, what if he dies ?' Codin whispered. 'Let's send Jon to get the doctor from the village nearby, at least then there will be two of you.'

'There is no time. By all means send Jon but meantime this one will die.. I am going to talk and explain to the parents. I'll go along with their decision.'

The father was the primary school teacher. He understood the risks and was all for it. But the mother said: 'Please let him die in peace if God so decided'. There was no time to argue; the child lost consciousness. The father cried, 'Please save my son!' Myra took out from her bag a large bore needle and quickly inserted it in the middle of the neck just below the Adam's apple. She removed the rod that cleaned the inside of the needle. A thin trickle of air went through and the child's breath came back, not good, not strong, but enough for him to open his eyes.The trouble was that the needle got blocked frequently and had to be unblocked. Then Jon returned with Doumi (his real name was Dr Doumitrescou) who came prepared with a cannula, a surgical blade and dressings, so that Myra was able to complete the procedure. The child got some colour back in his cheeks and mother kneeled by his side begging him to stay still. It went well and eventually the ambulance arrived. Myra asked Lilly to go with the child to the hospital to keep him quiet and asked the ambulance crew to give Doumi a lift back to his surgery. When all was over, Myra felt her legs giving way from under her.

The boy survived as did so many others once penicillin supplies had been flown in and administered at speed. In the end an epidemic was officially declared which affected many

260

villages in the area as well as the neighbouring towns. Only one village escaped the epidemic and it was discovered that that village did not even have a doctor. For many years the health of that small village had been the responsibility of a very elderly male nurse who was barely literate and most people in the profession ridiculed, but the authorities were reluctant to dismiss as there was no one to replace him. He did not keep any records. That he admitted. Rather than bother with record keeping he gave all the village a dose of vaccine every year, whether they needed it or not. The result was that nobody caught diphtheria! Nobody laughed at him anymore.

37
PETRA THE GYPSY

The winter proved to be one of the coldest on record. Mountains of snow and ice isolated the village. The blizzards cut even the telephone lines. The horse had to be kept in the neighbours' stable all the time. They no longer had a horse; they had given it away to the newly formed cooperative.

At the beginning, the cooperative had been offered as a voluntary organisation and many villagers joined it. It made sense to them to remove the boundaries and share the new tractor and the seeds promised, on the understanding that each would receive a proportion of the harvest according to the amount of land they had put in and their effort. Many others were reluctant to part with their land, which had been fought for by their parents and grandparents. Many had become landowners as late as 1907 after a heavily fought revolt in which many lives were lost.

The hackney could no longer be of use, a sledge would have been more appropriate. Myra had to make a lot of visits on foot. It was so cold, her cheeks got white with frost within minutes of walking, her eyelashes heavy and white and she had to blink often to prevent their sticking together. Her nose kept running defying the elements. On the advice of the midwife, Codin and Lilly and Myra started wearing men's socks on top of their boots to keep themselves from falling down on the slipery pathays. Evenings were long and heavy, the gas lamp tiring to the eye. Myra started spending more time with Theodora. It was much warmer in her room. Even Florian gave up sleeping outside and made his bed behind the stove. There was no work in those winter months; the village was hibernating. Only the women kept going, cooking, washing, looking after their children and doing all the jobs for which they could not find time during the summer and spring months. Theodora got the ancient loom out and started weaving little rugs out of colourful rags she had gathered during the year. Myra, not having anything else to do, started to take an interest. At first she cut old rags and bits of fabric into thin strips to help the old woman, then she started on Theodora's advice to sew them together in long ribbons. Theodora skilfully threaded the loom with long vertical strings of thick cotton or jute, then 'fed the spool' with the rags and started weaving. Fascinated, Myra felt inclined to try her hand at weaving and soon she was able to take over and had produced a few rugs to cover the dirt floors. She thought she would take one home to show off her new skills but then she felt they would only laugh at her. On other evenings she visited Lyna next door to help the girls with French and maths. In return, Lyna taught her how to turn the white fluffy lamb's wool into a yarn. Myra found it much harder to turn the spindle with a flick of the hand and make it spin round and round till the yarn gained the right thickness and strength. She thought that if she learned how to do it, she could join the other women on a summer Sunday afternoon when they gathered to gossip, sing and joke while with their fingers busily worked the wool or embroidered the fine shirts. Some evenings Myra spent at the Nitzulescous. The old teacher was fond of newspapers even if they were a week old and Myra brought Free Romania and the Literary Gazette every time she came back from Bucharest. Sometimes another friend of his joined them and they played 'tabinet' a simple game of cards. The time passed quicker that way and Myra slowly was warming up to the village and its life.

Then Myra met Petra, the only Gypsy in the village. She was famous for being able to read the future in the dregs of coffee and able to do a good massage. It was said about her that she could diagnose pneumonia by putting a raw egg on someone's back and sliding it about. If the egg started to fry on a certain spot that was where the chest infection was. No stethoscope required! She lived in a small, tidy house, alone except for the company of her goat. Her only son who was a musician, a fiddler, always away performing at weddings or christenings or dances on village greens visited her from time to time. Myra went to her occasionally to have a massage and to relax and on one such occasion could not resist the temptation of having her future read. Petra looked deep into Myra's eyes with her black, large eyes so that Myra felt as though they were burning into her. They drank Turkish coffee in a small cup each, then turned the cup upside down and let the dregs drain in the shape of what the future might show. It was not good news and Petra looked troubled. She laid out the cards as well. The same worried look remained on her face and Myra felt a hollow grow inside her.

'You will get news from your nearest and dearest.' 'Yeah, all right, just what I had expected her to say' Myra thought.

'The year ahead is bleak. Evil forces are fighting each other, the moon is going to be eaten by fire dragons, their curse will be upon us!'

'Oh good lord, what rubbish!' Myra could not help herself thinking, although deep down she wondered what was the meaning of all that. 'Soon you will be with child,' Petra continued after a pause, but then she became restless; she started rubbing her hands then shuffled the cards again.

'What is it, Petra? Come on, say it!'

'Oh, those cards sometimes go wild, they give me muddled messages.'

'Come on now, you've made me curious. Don't worry, I am a big girl. I would know what to believe.'

'A child appears in his coffin. It may be yours or not, I cannot say.'

Myra shuddered, then she composed herself. 'I would not worry Petra, all this is can't be true. We - my husband and I - do not plan on having children till I move back to Bucharest. Perhaps, what you see in the cards is to do with the poor children who died recently in the village'

'Yes, maybe, but you will be with child soon.'

Myra thought she was saying this because she knew she was married. Then Petra stopped. She said she'd lost the thread and would say no more. An atmosphere of darkness and unease fell in the room. After a while, Myra asked whether there were any sign of a long journey in those cards. Petra became a little less gloomy and shuffled the cards again. 'You yearn for a journey but that is a long, long way off. Many things will happen before that happens.'

Myra left and she became aware of a nagging headache which started behind her righr eye and found its way to the head. She was sick on her way back.

When she reached home Theodora had just finished her dinner. 'My, whatever happened, Missus Doctor? Why you looking so pale? Are you sickening for something?'

'No, Theodora, I went to see Petra, she gave me a good massage, then I had the foolish idea of asking her to read my coffee dregs. I don't know what happened but I feel sick.'

'You, a learned woman, a Doctor, to believe in such foolish things! I would not go near her, she casts a spell on people. Would you like something to drink?'

'Oh, perhaps a cup of tea would be nice, have you still some of that mint?'

'Yes, the water's just boiled in the kettle.'

Myra went to bed with the warm tea. 'Never, ever again will I go through this,' she promised herself. The next day she washed herself with melted snow, put her boots on and went to start a new day.

It was to be her birthday soon and, weather

permitting, Sanda, Adrian, Dumi and Cornel, Aurora and Basil were coming to celebrate. Cornel promised to bring his gramophone with the old records his father gave to him as a present. Dan said he was coming as well as long as the trains were working. So there they were on that bitterly cold February day when the stones cracked with the frost and the windows were covered with frosty stars, drinking plum brandy and listening to   'Zaraza, Beautiful Zaraza

Your black eyes never left me' and
'Sweet Bucharest Girls
You won't find others in all the world'
and then.

'Last night I've dreamt of you
and I woke up in tears
I thought you left me
And had forgotten me.'

Voices long forgotten from the past came through the gramophone spiced with the crackles of the old records. They found the old romantic verses hilarious and danced with their hands on their chests or on their foreheads in poses of the old silent movie actresses and actors.

38
STATISTICS

The winter slowly passed, the village totally isolated by the snow, was now engulfed in mud with impassable roads. Following the large amount of money invested in limiting the diphtheria epidemic, supplies of medicines, utensils and fodder for the horse were slow to come and grossly reduced in quantity. It reached the point that when going on a home visit Myra ask the farmer, 'While I am seeing to your father - and I will examine your child as well - could you please feed the horse? We are a bit short of food for him.'

The antibiotics supply dwindled away, painkillers and ulcer healing drugs were used up. In winter the demand was greater than ever. In the end Myra advised Codin to return the horse and the hackney to the Centre. The poor animal was in danger of dying of cold and starvation as the farmers changed their good will little by little since they had heard they were to be forced to join the cooperative and their land was to be taken away. The early spring proved moody as it always was. One day there was sunshine and the air felt pleasantly warm, then out of the blue sky, another snow shower and overnight frost. It brought with it new worries.

At the end of March, Zena, a poor woman who suffered from pellagra, unexpectedly gave birth to triplets. She was not due to give birth till the end of May, according to the midwife's calculations.

She was visiting her regularly and gave her a supply of vitamins. She advised her to get some rest but the husband kept telling her off and asking the midwife to leave his wife be. She had work to do. Myra called the ambulance, then went to the house and together with the midwife covered the babies, one boy and two girls, in cotton wool and asked the husband to build the fire up. They died quietly one after the other. None of them was alive when the ambulance finally arrived. The mother was distressed but she bore her grief in silence. The father said he was relieved: three mouths less to feed. Myra wanted to tell him if he had stopped drinking and done a little more work, sparing his poor wife, the outcome might have been different. But she said nothing. There was no point. It then dawned on her that these three deaths and the previous eight month old who died of pneumonia shot her infant mortality rate right up beyond the 5% limit! She wondered if these tragic events were to have any repercussions on her or the practice.

Back at the surgery Codin and a distraught midwife were waiting for her return. Codin started speaking. He cleared his throat and started: 'In the circumstances, I think we shall wait. If the father agrees not to declare the babies, and I will have a word with him-' he said, winking conspiratorially, 'we should declare the babies stillborn. After all, they were not due.' Myra said that was not an option, she had already spoken to the hospital paediatrician and the ambulance came to fetch the live babies. Under no circumstances was she going to do that. Sleepless nights followed. The worst was not knowing what would happen. After a week of not having heard from anyone, the anxiety died down and things returned to normal. Then a letter arrived asking Myra and the midwife to attend the Council meeting for the end of quarter year report. Finally the dreaded moment had arrived. Myra tried hard to concentrate on what she was doing but her thoughts kept twisting and turning to what she would say if she was asked about the triplets. The night seemed much longer than usual and sleep just did not happen. Mixed thoughts, mixed scenarios one more disturbing than another, passed through her mind. And from time to time Petra's eyes appeared out of nowhere only to be brushed away as superstitious rubbish.

The day came and she went to Mihaeshti where she met with the midwife. Her eyes were red and she smelled strongly of fermented wine, so Myra decided that whatever happened, she must not let her speak. The council hall was full. Doctors, nurses, people from the Infection Control Department, hospital staff, and at the desk on a stage, all the dignitaries: party political reps, the man with high boots, the county mayor, the Chief Officer of health and a few other 'boots' she did not recognise.

Dr Pica presented the report. It did not sound good. One of the boots hit the desk hard with his fist and started shouting that this was a disgrace and the doctors whose training was paid for by the hard working class had neglected their duty and had not fulfilled the tasks directly given by the party and its leader and he demanded that each of the non-achievers give a personal account and justify their negligence. One by one people were asked to stand up and explain. When Myra's name came up she took a time to respond. She was shaking and had to steady herself. She looked around her seeking to meet some sympathy in the eyes of her colleagues, some encouragement, but they averted their eyes and bowed their heads. There she stood, in front of all those eyes, trying to explain that the woman was a relic of the previous regime, malnourished and poor, that the babies came before they were due and lacking the means to save them they died. The roads were impassable and the ambulance took ages to arrive. What she had to say came out all wrong and shaky as she was frequently interrupted and her words were twisted by the officials, who brushed away her arguments as feeble excuses and in the end made her accept responsibility for everything that had happened and undertake the commitment that in future it would not happen again. One after another, people stood up and each was humiliated and made to 'auto criticise' and make promises they knew they could not keep. If a few tried to be more outspoken they met with the menacing reply: 'Are you trying to make our government responsible? The party and our leader have done so much for us'! They had had to lower their gaze and accept. They went back to their villages and Myra for the first time accepted George's words: 'We need to get out of here, the

271

sooner the better.' There is no hope! Not so long ago, the spring before, I was the saint who saved lives and now I am guilty and responsible for mistakes that had nothing to do with me.

39
THE SAINT

It was a day of early, long awaited spring which came without warning. One day frost covered the bare trees and the dirt road was moulded by cart wheels and horses' hooves and track tyres into hard shiny shapes; the next, the heavy sky opened and the roads turned into deep mud. There was a sense of hope in the air, smoke stopped coming out of chimneys, people came out in heavy rubber boots making slow progress through the sticky deep mud. The surgery lost its freezing coldness. Poor Jon, the caretaker, did not have to light the fire at the crack of dawn in the heavy stove which took ages to get warm.

Myra opened the door to the waiting room, said good morning and asked Codin to stop telling the people off for bringing mud into the waiting room; they could not help it, they could not leave their boots and galoshes at the door as someone would be bound to steal them.

It must have been almost midday when the midwife burst into the room without even knocking.

'Doctor ,doctor! Come quick!' Codin followed the midwife, trying to stop her. A patient was sitting on the chair with the blood pressure cuff still attached to her upper arm. 'Please, she is bleeding to death, we are bound to go to prison!' The midwife was actually crying. Myra was thinking, 'Has she been drinking? Why is her nose so red? From tears or cold or drink? Codin came

273

in and took charge. Within seconds he had cleared the waiting room and told everyone to go home and come back later.

'Now, let's get this story straight,' he said, while Myra was becoming increasingly concerned as the story unfolded. The midwife had delivered the baby but, she confessed between crying fits, the placenta was late to come out and for some reason she pulled on the umbilical cord, which tore short and the mother began to bleed heavily. The placenta was not going to come out. Myra's heart missed at least a couple of beats. She realised that she did not know much about retained placentas. Obstetrics were not her forte. She had been part of a a large group of students in the hospital maternity ward and the consultant preferred to do the work himself rather than leave it to mere students to have a go. How sorry she was now that she had not done some night shifts when she could have gained personal experience.

Every maternal death would be heavily punished morally and materially. The first thought was that she wanted to run away but she knew that she could not. Then, she felt hatred towards the midwife, the system, everything. After that she calmed down and started to think logically. There was no way they could take the carriage through the mud, they would certainly have got stuck, so they went on foot. One foot in front of the other, tons of mud attached to the boots slowed the advance. Progress was slow and Myra hoped the wretched mother was still alive. Just before leaving she went to her lodgings and put into her bag, besides a few injections and surgical gloves,, the Obs. & Gyne book she had studied during her happy student days. There was a chapter she could see in front of her eyes called 'Obstetrical Hints and Guide to Procedures'. She could see the title but not, unfortunately, the contents. The fact that the midwife kept repeating, 'Oh my God, Sweet Jesus, the police will be there,' did not do Myra any good. She finally arrived, wet and full of mud. Men were standing around in the yard, their fur hats low over foreheads, their shoulders bent against the rain, some smoking heavy rollups cigarettes. The father of the child was pacing to and fro, a bottle of plum brandy, by the smell in the air, was doing the rounds.

Myra and the midwife walked into the dimly lit room teeming with women of all ages, the air thick with their breath. She could not see the patient in the crowd. The dim grey light came through a window too small and too high in the wall. Myra got angry. What was this? Were they trying to kill the woman? Did they not have any sense? She turned to the midwife and said, 'Stop whining, just clear the room!'

Only at that moment could she see a very old woman sitting on the floor holding a up bundle in her arms wrapped up in a shawl and next to her a young woman, collapsed. The floor was covered in straw mixed with blood, red and brown. On this bed of straw the woman, so pale that even her hair appeared white, with her legs sprawled open, a river of red blood gushing from her lay there unmoving and unconscious. Myra took a couple of deep breaths, determined not to faint. She had fainted in the surgical theatre when she did her first D&C and had embarrassed herself. That put her off obstetrics and gyne for ever. She barked at the midwife, 'Take the baby out of here, and open the window!' The stink of blood was getting at her. She kneeled beside the woman and touched her. She was flaccid and unresponsive and so young... she was probably the same age as Myra, her early twenties. She had to do something, while her pulse was present and her heart still beating. She opened her bag and brought the book out and propped it against the wall above the woman's head and opened it at the relevant page. She put surgical gloves on, cursing in in her mind that they were two sizes larger than her hands. She felt suddenly calm, all the fear vanished and there was nothing or anyone else, just the patient and she. Myra examined her, but she did not react in any way. her pulse grew weaker and weaker. There was no way that she could push and deliver the placenta on her own. For a while Myra stopped and calmly did nothing but read the procedure from the book, deaf to the sobs and words of the midwife urging her to do something. The book said: 'Enter the uterine cavity from the right side, gently examine the surface of the placenta. Aim for the upper right horn and gently displace the placenta with minimal pressure. ' She followed the instructions step by step and the whole baby house came out with a loud plop. Myra's face was sprinkled with blood and she could taste it in her mouth. That was all, that was the end. Myra stood motionless besides the mother, who was still breathing. After a time that seemed years the blood slowed to a trickle and then stopped altogether. It was so quiet you could cut the silence with a knife. The woman lay with her eyes closed but she was still alive. Somewhere the baby was whimpering.

The thought of giving her blood crossed Myra's mind and she was thinking how she could cross match some blood. Then, she had an idea to ask the older men who had served in the war if they knew their blood group. Suddenly the woman stirred. She briefly opened her eyes and went back to sleep. Myra called her mother in and kneeled beside her again. 'Water', the young mother whispered. In no time the midwife returned with a bowl of water and her mother came back with a steaming bowl of hot soup. Myra just stood, watching how the mother fed the woman spoon after spoon of hot soup. The midwife brought the baby in and the young mother gave a smile, so beautiful, so satisfied, so complete, before going back to sleep, this time a restful recuperating sleep. Myra stood up and took her blood-soaked gloves off slowly, slowly taking great care that her shaking legs should not give way and buckle under her, put the book in the bag and walked out, leaving instructions for the midwife to check the baby and the placenta and return to the surgery. She then turned to the old woman and asked for some water to wash the blood off her face and hands.

It was still raining but the large crowd of men, women, family and neighbours was still out in the yard. Myra was about to apologise for shouting at them when, before she could open her mouth, the crowd parted in two columns to let her pass, bowing low. She could almost see the tops of their fur hats and dark shawls. Some were signing from forehead to chest from right to left, the sign of the cross, some moved forward and grabbed her hand to kiss it. She pulled her hands away, embarrassed. That was all she needed! She was so tired.

Outside Jon was waiting with the carriage; he had made it after all and Myra was grateful. He said, 'What happened, Doctor? They are all talking about you. They say the woman was dying but that you read to her from the Holy Book and she came back from the dead. They say you must be a saint!'

Little by little the spring came, with the earth waking up from the long frozen winter, with little buds on the trees and signs of renewed activity calmed the spirits and the practice returned to everyday activity but the fear and resentment never left Myra. She could barely stand Emilian's voice in the nights when he came home shouting, among curses directed at every one: 'Doctor, you are a yid! Tell us you are a yid!' Before, she used to lift her shoulders and shrug it off, pick up a book and bury her head in the plot or listen to the commotion of Lyna and the children coming over the fence. Now it was intolerable. Nor could she put up with her fear when the Party Instructor on occasions - although not very often - would get drunk and come at night to the gate calling her name. 'Doctor', he would shout: 'Come out, I have something to tell you!' Myra would stay very still listening to her heart pounding faster and faster, cover her ears and pray the nonsense would soon stop. But on and on it went until Florian, wakened from his slumber would go to the gate and in his quiet voice ask him to go away and sleep it off and let everybody else sleep in peace. The next day all would be quiet, as if it had never happened.

Myra had a chat with Anna Pica the next time they met at a quiet moment and Anna advised her to let it pass, to say nothing. The world they lived in was not ready to take sides against authority and overcome prejudices. Sound advice, Myra had to agree; if she made too much noise they could start digging into the files and find out she had married into a family of dissidents and that her own father had just been released from prison, and everyone could be put at risk. Besides, by that time she had found out she was pregnant. Dan was beside himself with joy. Myra had her doubts. She thought it was not a good time and with the morning sicknessas well, she was not very pleased. She remembered Petra's words but quickly dismissed her from her mind.

40
DISASTER

For the first time mass immunisation against polio was set in motion. The oral Sabin strain vaccine was for the first time produced in the Soviet Union. A directive came with instructions that the vaccine sugar coated tablets had to be kept at a temperature of not warmer than four degrees C. That meant it had to be put on ice and Seaca did not have an icebox. Codin was sent to investigate. He found a cellar full of ice at a wine grower's in a nearby village. Lilly and Jon and the midwife all were sent to mobilise people of all ages door to door.

On the day, the activity started early. Long queues had formed. People knew what a dreadful illness polio was - most had relatives who had been affected by it or had died - and came to be immunised. They eagerly awaited the arrival of the vaccine. Codin brought two buckets full of ice ready to receive it. The boxes finally arrived. Boxes a hundred doses each were packed in square cardboard cartons which contained sugar coated pink pills. Codin put all the boxes on ice.One pill given to each person. After about an hour Lilly noticed the cartons getting soggy in the melting ice and the water which dripped from it turning pale pink. She came to report and Myra took a new box from the bottom of the pile. The box, softened by the water, split open and suddenly there were pills everywhere, some with the sugar coat half melted showing signs of disintegration. Myra cursed herself for being so stupid, she should have   had some sense.   Jon went next door and came back with a couple of jars and all the staff started crawling on all fours, picking the pills off the floor as quickly as they could. They did not utter a single sound nor did they explain the interruption to the waiting crowd.They continued giving them pills as soon as they came off the floor while Lilly was put in charge of removing all the carton packaging and transferring the contents into   jars. Myra and Codin went outside   and started giving each person the vaccine in their mouths with all the speed they could muster half pink half white fearing that the pills melt altogether. Codin was determined not to pay another fine for the lost vaccine which had happened because of the poor quality of packaging and lack of adequate storring in proper ice bags. What they did not admit was their oun lack of proper planning and reasoning. They acted like automatons, it was not always someone else's fault. To   cover   it   up   they continued with the vaccination of at least a large part of the people of a usless vaccine. Codin said so to Myra and this time she agreed. What was the point of being honest in such a dishonest society? At least the great majority received good vaccine and the tame live virus in the vaccine would soon spread into the community and destroy the killer viruses.

The task accomplished, the following Saturday Myra went home to Bucharest for a well-deserved break. Having dispensed with the hackney and horse that she had used for transport she acquired a donkey and a cart, after Jon's intense negotiations with a farmer. It was not too bad. Myra did not complain although the donkey had a tendency to stop in mid journey or refuse to start unless Jon coaxed him with a carrot attached at the end of a stick which he held firmly in front of the donkey's eyes. That is how she travelled the five kilometres to the train station. Once in the train with all her heavy luggage, containing four chickens, a number of large round bread loaves, large lump of cheese and two dozen eggs, all occupying a suitcase and a basket, she settled down, happy to have found a seat in the packed compartment. She was still wearing thick trousers as the weather continued to be changeable and in her lap she held on tightly to her handbag and the portable radio she always carried with her. She closed her eyes for a little rest. She was so tired; the morning sickness and the rush with the vaccine had all left her quite exhausted.

She had dozed off when a sharp pain in her lower abdomen woke her up with a jolt. The pain did not last very long but a few minutes later another wave of pain, this time lasting longer, bent her over. The colicky pains repeated themselves and then Myra felt hot fluid coming through her trousers and she knew she was having a miscarriage.

She looked around her and all her travelling companions were young men, most likely coming home from work. She made up her mind to sit tight let them all descend at theirr destination, she

282

would be the last to leave the compartment. She hoped Dan would be on the platform to greet her. Another wave of intense pain made her bend over and hold her breath. 'Are you all right, Miss?' The man next to her asked. 'Oh yes ,thank you,' Myra replied.

The derelict outskirts and industrial sites of Bucharest appeared and Myra was praying she would make it home. She became aware of a white light. People dressed in white with their heads covered in white bonnets glided soundlessly round her. There were white-painted bars at her feet on which a chart was clipped . Her head was spinning, her mouth was dry and she was thirsty. 'Please, where am I? Can I have a drop of water?' she said in a weak voice. She could barely hear it herself.

A nurse appeared, an elderly woman all dressed in white. 'You are in Grivitza Hospital, you came in last night,' she said.

'Hospital,? What am I doing here?' Myra asked as she became quite agitated and attempted to sit up. And then came the memory of pain and the realisation of what had happened hit her.

'Hello, friend, it is nice to see you and what's more to see you alive!' a male voice said and Mircea, a colleague from her med. school appeared by her side. He was an intern in gynaecology at this hospital.

'How did I come here? Myra asked. 'All I remember is I was on a train coming home from my practice when that awful pain started.'

'A man brought you in,' the nurse spoke.

'He found you collapsed next to him in a train, and he did not know anything about you.' He thought it was women's problems and the quickest way was to bring you here in a taxi.'

'Where is my bag, my radio?'

'He did not mention bags or radio, we have not received anything from him'

'Mircea, have I lost my baby?'

'Yes, I am afraid you have' he said, squeezing Myra's hand' Your husband telephoned, he is coming later. Tomorrow we are planning a D&C to clear all the remnants.'

Myra said nothing. She turned on her side, away from them and closed her eyes to sleep. The remnants, that was all that remained from the baby who had inhabited her body for a few months. Even though she did not plan it, she grew used to it and fed him with her body. Sleep did not come. A sort of numbness came instead, an immobility. All signs of life seemed to desert her. Curled up in foetal position, she could think of nothing, feel nothing. She just remained there, cocooned in darkness. She did not hear Dan, nor did she smell the scent of the flowers he brought. If he talked to her she did not register his voice. It may have been a day or two until he came to take her home. Once there, Myra went into the little bedroom and straight into bed. Dan spoke quietly to her but she waved him away. Silky brought in biscuits and tea, touched her forehead and left the room. Only Azeb, the dog, took no heed and curled up next to her in bed. All was quiet.

Myra felt a deep emptiness somewhere inside

her, a sense of loss. Although her reasonable inner self reminded her she had never wanted a baby, that it was better at this stage in their life not to be tied down with children, she was screaming inside, her heart breaking from sorrow. In the quietness of the room tears began to run and then she cried out loud. Screams of loss followed. She was howling like a wounded animal. Dan entered the room and held her tight till the flow of sorrow mixed with anger, loss, defeat abated.

Myra remained in that state of prostration for a few more days. Then she suddenly remembered and got up and asked Dan if he knew the person who took her to the hospital.

'You do not know? You did not ask? He saved my life!'

'I thought you knew that person.' Dan replied. 'It did not cross my mind that the kind person in possession of all your belongings was not known to you. I was so shocked by the news I did not think to ask There is no way to find him now. If he introduced himself I did not hear him. I am so sorry'

Myra tried to remember what that man looked like, but the only memory of him was that he was young, perhaps the same age as she was, and that he wore a French navy beret.

'Perhaps you will meet him in the train someday,' Dan said.

Myra gradually regained her composure and asked for a drink. At that moment Silky entered the room . She looked at the two of them joined in a tight embrace and in a quiet voice announced: 'Your mother is here.' Behind her in the door frame stood Esther. Like in a movie, Myra still recalls, how Esther walked in without a word, opened her arms and closed them round Myra .

41
COMPULSION

The days that early summer of 1963 somehow became longer and heavier. Everything became a chore. Colleagues and friends still came visiting once in a while but Myra lost her enthusiasm. Somehow nothing satisfied her. She found solace perhaps only in her cigarettes. She continued with her visits and the surgery, she went to the fields to tend to injured men and women, she shared with them the simple meals which the women brought at midday from home in their little baskets, bread, cheese and onions and a pitcher of water spread out on a clean cheese cloth. She listened with half an ear to what they were saying, all the while wishing she were somewhere else. Where? She did not rightly know. The only thing that cheered her up a little were the two white feathered turkeys which knocked at her window early in the morning reminding her there was another day. And of course, demanding to be fed. The relatives came visiting: her sister Bea, Dan 's sister Amy, they had a lovely time. Bea was all excited because that year she was going to start her university course at the School of Architects.

Myra became aware she was pregnant again. This time it was what she wanted, perhaps she could not accept defeat, perhaps it was because for the first time she had experienced the void of personal loss. Myra also realised something that she previously never thought about, just took it for granted: having children is not a God given right to everyone; that one should have a child no matter what the obstacles or material circumstances dictate; a time to have a child may never be right. This time she was more cautious. She took her annual leave. She was entitled to two weeks holiday a year. She went to Bucharest and consulted her good friend Cathryn who was a well- known gynaecologist. All was well with the pregnancy and Dan and Myra went to Constanza. They both needed a holiday. They met old friends, Lya, Spiros and all the rest of the crowd, and had a good time and her mood lightened. In spite of the morning sickness, she returned to Seaca in better spirits.

That summer there was a total eclipse of the moon. On the radio there was no talk of anything else. The general advice was to avoid looking directly at the sun as it disappeared behind the black moon and it left the world in darkness. Myra started to spread the message but she was met with indifference. The village men went about their business as usual saying that they would spend that day indoors. The women shook their heads knowingly:

'Now we will have to pay for our sins! The time has come! Remember Petra's words? The old gypsy did not lie!'

No matter how hard Myra tried to convince them that this was a natural phenomenon, that it had nothing to do with dragons or any other supernatural vengeful creatures intent on eating the sun, that this was a simple moment in the casual encounter of the moon and the sun, that every 18 years or thereabouts the moon passes in front of the sun and everything turns impenetrable black. They shook their heads in the firm belief they knew better. Myra continued to tell them not to look directly at the sun or they may get blind.

Petra, forever Petra! The power of the gypsy woman had over the minds – including Myra's!. Did she not lose the baby just as Petra had predicted? Here she was pregnant again and she could not help a shiver of fear passing over her in spite of all reason and logic.

The eclipse lasted almost half an hour and the beautiful golden crown started appearing behind the moon as if a celestial fire was caressing and dispersing the dark round moon. Slowly the moon moved away, revealing more and more of the sun in its light and brightness. The village was silent but for the church bells which rang continually. Myra watched with Codin and the Nitzulescus through dark shades, all fears dispersed by the beautiful images.

Everybody returned to their activities and soon the event was forgotten. They were all too busy with the harvest, picking the grapes, cutting the corn and all their other activities.

Summer gone, the harvest in, the weather held out till all the hay was stored safely, and the grapes ripened. Celebrations took place in September on St Mary's and the day of the cross but, unlike the previous year, in a sombre mood.

Rumours had started that the farmers were going to lose their land. This time they could not get away from it. Petra's words came to haunt them again that autumn. A sad silence fell over the village once the harvest was over, fear polluting the air. The campaign of land collectivisation began in earnest and intensified with each day that passed. What had started as a voluntary affiliation became compulsory. The mayor, the Collective Agricola farm and the party rep joined forces and created a visiting committee. They had orders from the central governing party to achieve 99% of collectivisation by the end of the year. Myra was officially asked to join and be on hand should any medical help be required. The group knocked door to door to talk to the owners and persuade them to sign their land away to the new enterprise.

Myra felt that was not her job, she had come to the village to tend to the sick, not to get involved in party politics. However she was told in no uncertain terms that she had better join and do her duty as a citizen and party devotee. When she objected that such work interfered with the surgeries and the preventive work she was doing, she was advised to change her timetable and accommodate this important duty.

Myra wanted to argue some more but she thought better of it. She spoke to Dan and both agreed it was better not to attract attention to herself. She did not want the people in power to start asking questions like why she was no longer a member of the Socialist Youth Movement and why she had not applied to become a member of the party. God only knew, there were enough skeletons in both cupboards, hers and Dan's. Bringing all that to light would take her chances of ever winning a work place in Bucharest from minimal to nil. Besides she already had a black mark from the authorities regarding her infant mortality statistics and Myra remembered that only too well.

That way the daily march from gate to gate started. All the gates previously left ajar were closed tight, the dogs left loose in the yards. The visiting group armed themselves with strong sticks. First they knocked at the gate with those sticks.–It took a while and repeated knocks till someone finally showed up. The rosy future awaiting the owners was explained to them and the advantages of toiling on the land together. Some people maintained traditional hospitality and tied the dogs and asked the group in for all the family to hear what they had to say. Some farmers, after repeated knocks, send out the man of the family to hear what the group had to say. Others did not answer at all. Those were marked to be visited again on the following day. To start with, the conversations between the officials and the farmers were civil, they exchanged greetings, then the president of the collective outlined his plans. Joining forces with grain given by a central government store and modern machinery sounded very encouraging. Myra kept quiet and listened. But the farmers, with the inherent peasant's mistrust, wanted to know more: would the land remain their property? what would happen when the owner of the land died? who was going to inherit? could they keep the papers and pass on the land to the children? The mayor intervened, looking uneasy, and from what the party rep was saying it did not sound like good news. Yes, the wife will get an income as long as she put in days' work. What about the children, they asked. What if the wife or their elders, who owned the land in the first place, were ill or could not work? They got the same shifting answer. The yields would be distributed according to the days worked. But the yelds will be so much better, the president of the collective hastened to add, with all those new improvements there will be plenty for everyone. No, there was no right of inheritance. Why would they have to inherit and return to burgeois practice of possession, when they grew up in a socialist state, and were looked after and given a good education. Besides, if they continued to work the land they would earn, just like their parents.

Others asked what will happen to their horses, oxen, ploughs? They will become the property of the collective was the answer.

The farmers scratched their heads. Very few among the poorest signed straight away, most said they would pass on the message to the rest of the family, and would consider. The group left but they were back the next day.

Myra noticed a change of mood in the village. Before, everyone greeted her with smiles when she passed by, she was their saint, after all, but now when the women looked at her Myra felt the daggers in their eyes. She had joined the ranks of the enemy.

Her sleep became disturbed. She was waking up tired. She started surgery one hour earlier to allow time for all her duties. Attendance at the surgery became visibly less, especially the response to vaccinations or follow up. They had diminished dramatically, which was such a worry. When Myra tried to smile and enquire about a member of the family whom she had already met, either she was not given an answer or the answer was momosyllabic. That was not fair, it broke her heart. She felt lonely and abandoned. She touched her growing tummy as if to seek reassurance and comfort from the growing embryo.

The visiting official group hardened the tone of their conversations. The exchanges became more threatening. When they talked to poorer farmers the president of the collective reminded them of the bitter times when they worked for landowners who spent their time in Paris or Berlin all year round, leaving the land in the hand of the *arendash*, the administrator, who exploited the workers and cheated on them and lined their own pockets. The farmers replied that now they had their land they intended to make good for themselves. The party man, with his high boots, replied this was not the way the country was going, that people had a civil duty and that the party knew the people needed to be brought out from their miserable practices to progressive ways. The farmers threatened that if they continued to refuse, their land would be taken anyway and in exchange they would be given another plot at the edge of the collective. The farmers who were better off and had more land were approached differently. They were reminded they were *chiabouri*, part of the bourgeoisie. They should be thankful that they were not in prison as enemies of the people.

Myra kept her head down. She stepped in only when someone felt unwell. At one point, the man everyone called Uncle Stan fell to the ground suddenly and lost consciousness. Myra stepped in to give him mouth to mouth resuscitation and he regained consciousness but he could not move. An ambulance was called but Stan had suffered a major stroke and died next day at the Roshiori Hospital. He was only in his forties and left behind a wife and children and an elderly mother and father. That stopped the visiting programme till after the funeral. The atmosphere became very tense.

Soon, the visiting group restarted their activities. More people signed their land away. One day Zamphira, the widow, disappeared. That day Myra was late in joining the group. There were two patients who took her time as they developed jaundice. She had to deal with urine samples and blood samples and send them to Draganesti Hospital. For safety, she had to talk to the family and explain the dangers of hepatitis and how they must avoid sharing cutlery, and plates as well as towels with the patients till results came through from the lab. In those days diagnosis was based on liver function tests and urine test as well as inspecting stools and urine. Australia hep A virus was not as yet heard of.

When she joined the visiting party there was a gathering in Zamphira's yard. The gate was wide open and her hens were running loose in the road. The door to her dwelling was wide open; only her dog was guarding the entrance, howling. The neighbours were searching everywhere: indoors, outdoors, the yard, the fields but there was no sign of her. Somebody suggested she mightt have run away to her sister who was living in another village. Only the day before she had argued with the party rep telling him he should be ashamed of himself for what he and his mates were doing to the people. She was outspoken,, Zamphira. She had lived on her own for the last twenty years. Her husband had been declared missing in the war. She had one boy who left the village early and worked somewhere in a town nobody knew of. Only the day before Zamphira told them all her land was fought for, she being descended from Avram Iancou, a freedom fighter who led a rebellion against oppression a century before. She had inherited the land from her husband, who gave his life for that land and his country and his forefather was given the land after the 1907 rebellion, and she was not going to sign any papers. Myra had stayed behind to calm her down but, Zamphira did not seem to listen to her. There was hostility mounting around the visiting group and they decided to call it a day and go home. Three days later they found Zamphira at the bottom of the deep narrow well.

After that, most of the people were subdued. They gave in and signed. Only about six families held onto their rights and were given alternative plots on the periphery of the collective, where land was infertile and full of stones.

Myra spent more time indoors after surgery. Theodora kindly looked after her. The Rogoveanous and Emilian were among the first to accept the collective. Emilian was the miller and he wanted to keep his job, and Florian could not care less about what was going on. The Nitzulescous signed as well, they did not want any trouble. They did not have children and they had a pension from his teaching days.

Myra spent more time in the village. She preferred not to travel. Esther came on a visit and brought news from Focsani. Usher had found a job in a factory which assembled wooden barrels and he was happy, smiling as usual, Anca had finally graduated and was sent to work in a mountain village near Focsani. Esther heard from Lilliana who had married an elderly colonel and moved to Bucharest. Dan came visiting every week and at one time he brought his mother with him. Silky was full of news of Lydia's engagement. She had finally given up Miron, her sweetheart and agreed to marry the son of a friend of the family. Poor Lydia, Myra thought. She wondered how Lydia could go through with it.

The village returned to the daily routine. The grapes were made into wine and the plums into plum brandy and that improved the mood of everybody. Rather unexpectedly, Geta, one of the women who some years back had an argument with Myra, came to say she was getting married and she was wondering if 'Mister Engineer' and Myra would be witnesses. Myra felt uneasy, it was a difficult situation. She said she would speak to the visiting priest. She went to meet him and disclosed to him for the first time that she was Jewish. The priest said it did not matter, the ceremony would be brief and if Dan accepted that would be enough. His own wife would take Myra's place when the crowns were put on the bride's and groom's heads. The wedding went well and a lot of people came to celebrate, fed up with all the gloom of recent events. A *taraph* of gypsy musicians came, tables and benches were set out on the village green, the wine and the fiddler's music soared in the rhythm of the *tzamball* and everybody had a good time.

'World, world sister world
That's the world, passing by
Some are born and some die.. '
The words of Maria Tanase resounded also
'Stop crying dear bride '
In the evenings Myra started studying. There was an examination coming up. It was a bit hard to memorise all the teaching, when her head was so full of recent events and the pregnancy was not having a good effect on her brain. She was not successful and did not get one of the six places available in Bucharest. She decided she would try again at the next session of examinations.

The good news was that her friend and neighbour Doumi who had by then served four years in the village, got in. He got a place as a surgeon trainee in a Bucharest hospital. At the same time Dr Pica was promoted to the post of Medical Officer at regional level. and he was moving to Piteshti and of course Anna was going with him, having obtained a hospital training position in Paediatrics in the same town. Cornelius, Myra's friend, became the new County Medical Officer. That was a cause of celebration and all gathered at Myra's to celebrate. Myra had become heavier. Codin and Dan took charge of the preparations, the weather was still good and with Theodora's help they organised a barbecue. Chicken and a kid were slaughtered and grilled on wood brought from Bucharest. Then Cornelius put on the old gramophone and the old songs filled the rooms. They danced till the dust rose up from the dirt floor. Theodora brought in a bucket of water and a broom and sprinkled the water on the floor to settle the dust and they danced and drank some more.

Day followed day, growing shorter and shorter The gas lamp was lit earlier and earlier. Myra was studying and also knitting. There was no wool to buy in Bucharest and the country wool Lyna spun was too rough for baby clothes. But George found out that in Bucharest woolly scarves were available at the Laffayette stores and he queued up and bought a fair number. He was told they could be unpicked and knitted again, that was what most of the women did. So Myra unravelled the fine, soft wool and began knitting matinee jackets, boots and bonnets for the new baby. Of course George bought mostly blue scarves, he so wanted a grandson to carry the name, but Myra wanted a daughter and Dan said he was happy with whatever was coming.

Time came for maternity leave. She said goodbye to Codin and Jon, and Lilly and the midwife Rozalia, she embraced the Nitzulescous. Stephanie, her godchild came with her mother and Geta. She asked Theodora to take care of the turkeys, Dan would come later at the end of the year to collect them. Myra did not want to allow herself to think too much she would have started crying. Tears of affection and gratefulness gathered in her throat. Those years in the village seemed to her like a lifetime. Everybody wished Myra a happiness and a healthy infant. They kissed the back of her hand and they were going to wait for her safe return.

But Myra knew deep down that she would never come back. The future awaited.

Lightning Source UK Ltd.
Milton Keynes UK
UKOW06f2333231215

265291UK00001B/27/P